One thing is needful

One thing is needful

Rev. William MacLean

REFORMATION PRESS

2021

© 2021 by Reformation Press
11 Churchill Drive, Stornoway
Isle of Lewis, Scotland HS1 2NP

www.reformationpress.co.uk

Edited by Dr Robert J. Dickie and Dr Catherine E. Hyde
Cover design by Lucid Raccoon: info@lucidraccoon.co.uk

British Library Cataloguing-in-Publication Data
A catalogue record for this book is available from the British Library

ISBN numbers
Paperback   978-1-872556-50-5
Hardback   978-1-872556-51-2
E-book   978-1-872556-52-9

Contents

Introduction

THE Rev. William MacLean was ordained to the ministry in 1948 and served congregations of the Free Presbyterian Church in Scotland, New Zealand and Australia. The twelve sermons and lectures in this book were delivered during his New Zealand ministry, which was based in the North Island city of Gisborne and lasted from 1962 to 1973.

Mr MacLean's aim was to proclaim the whole counsel of God to his hearers. The sermons and addresses cover a variety of subjects and are characteristic of his discursive style of preaching, which included allusions to parallel passages of Scripture. In common with other Highland preachers, he also 'spiritualised' texts, with the intent of opening up the richness of Scripture and bringing his hearers to consider the salvation of their precious souls. As a faithful and loving pastor, Mr MacLean not only expounded Scripture but also taught his hearers to beware the false doctrines and inconsistent practices which characterised that era. Such teaching is necessary in every age.

Many people valued the recordings of Mr MacLean's sermons and addresses. Edward Greene of Oxford was among that number. He had been signally blessed under Mr MacLean's first ministry on the Isle of Lewis, and the

ONE THING IS NEEDFUL

two men became close personal friends.[1] Mr Greene arranged for recordings to be painstakingly transcribed by Cathie Mary MacIver of Carloway (previously of London), with a view to eventual publication. Typescripts were kindly passed to the publisher by Roy Middleton of the Barnoldswick Free Presbyterian congregation following Mr Greene's death, and these have been carefully prepared for publication by Dr Catherine Hyde. The publisher is grateful to all these individuals, and to others who have encouraged publication of this work. Scripture quotations are from the Authorised (King James) Version of the Bible, and rhymed versions of Psalms are from the Scottish Metrical Version of 1650.

The Rev. William MacLean passed to his eternal rest in 1985. The Rev. Donald MacLean of Glasgow wrote an obituary of his longstanding friend and ministerial colleague for the denominational magazine of the Free Presbyterian Church.[2] By courtesy of the magazine's present Editor, a lightly edited version of the obituary provides a biographical sketch of this worthy minister of the gospel.

In issuing this volume of sermons and addresses by the Rev. William MacLean, the publisher desires that the Lord would bless them to the souls of readers.

STORNOWAY
AUGUST 2021

---

[1] See 'Obituary: Mr Edward Greene (1937–2018)', *Free Presbyterian Magazine*, Vol. 125 (2020), pp. 242–250, written by the Rev. Douglas Somerset.
[2] 'The late Rev. William MacLean M.A., Ness', *Free Presbyterian Magazine*, Vol. 90 (1985), pp. 378–385.

Biographical sketch

WILLIAM MACLEAN was born in Lochcarron in 1907, where his father was a respected elder in the Free Church congregation. His mother, too, was a pious woman, and he was brought up to have a place and regard for the gospel. He was religiously inclined from his young days, and was not much given to the frivolities of youth. He often attended Communion services with his father, and had a particular delight in hearing sermons, being especially interested in preachers with their different ways of presenting the gospel.

He pursued his studies at Dingwall Academy and Glasgow University, where he graduated M.A. During these days his religious interest continued, together with his interest in preachers. During the time he was in Glasgow he stayed with Mr Thomas MacRae, who later became an elder in the congregation. William MacLean often attended St Jude's Free Presbyterian Church with the MacRae family, and came to have a very high regard for the Rev. Neil Cameron, the minister of that congregation. He was particularly impressed by the solemnity of Mr Cameron's preaching, and the convincing way he set forth the doctrines of the Word of God.

He was eventually appointed to a post in Lionel Public School in Ness, Isle of Lewis, in 1929, where he began his teaching career. When there, his interest in young people was shown by his forming a boys' club, in which his religious disposition was also shown by giving a lecture on the Sabbath. But he was destined to learn that this religious interest, his delight in ministers and sermons, and his high regard for a minister like Rev. Neil Cameron, were of no value for eternity, for, as the Saviour says, 'Marvel not that I said unto thee, Ye must be born again.'

He often paid visits to Glasgow, and on one occasion, on the April Communion Sabbath in 1932, he was at the evening service in St Jude's Church. The Rev. Neil Cameron had passed away to his eternal rest the previous March. The preacher on this particular occasion was the Rev. Donald Beaton, Oban, whose text was Luke 18:27. Mr MacLean's experience is better told by himself in a letter he wrote to a godly pastor in England:

> God's heritage has often been refreshed and edified by relating to one another what the Lord has done for their souls. 'Come,' said the Psalmist, 'and I will declare what he hath done for my soul.' God moves in a mysterious way, his wonders to perform. Some he gently draws into his blessed fold like Lydia, others in a startling and sudden manner like Paul and the Philippian jailor, brands plucked as it were in a moment from the burning. So it was in my own case, if I am truly one of the little flock.
>
> Religious after a manner, from my youth up, I was, on Monday morning, April 25th, 1932, cut down, stripped of all the fig leaves of a general profession, and brought in guilty before the Judge of all. On the previous evening I had heard a dear servant of Christ preach from the

words, 'The things which are impossible with men are possible with God' (Luke 18:27).

At the time neither the words nor the sermon made much of an impression on me. Often before I had trembled under the preaching of the Word, but not so that Sabbath evening. It was on the Monday forenoon that the words were applied with power, and the doctrines faithfully opened up in the sermon, of man's fall and his absolute inability to save himself, became awful realities to me. In the presence of the Holy One of Israel, in the light of his august majesty and the spirituality of his law, a strong conviction was wrought in my soul that by the works of the law no flesh can be justified. The door of escape by the covenant of works I saw to be closed and barred.

I then looked to the election of grace, and hoped that I might be of the number given to the Son before the foundation of the world, but here again no door of hope was given. Instead, a subduing view of God's sovereignty silenced all rebellious thoughts, calmly drawing all the faculties of the soul into a willing acquiescence of his justice. I believed myself to be a deserving and rightful heir of wrath, and thought that there and then I was to enter a lost eternity. But in my low state he thought upon me, because his mercy endureth for ever, and was pleased to reveal his Son in me. He spoke peace to my soul, and for a time I saw no man save Jesus only.

This event took place on that Monday morning in a railway carriage in which he was seated alone, travelling between Glasgow and Mallaig on his way back to recommence teaching. He then continued to write as follows:

A time of darkness soon followed. The fountains of corruption within appeared to have broken up, and the cry

11

of the Psalmist in the 51st Psalm was mine. Tossed thus with doubts and fears on the ocean of natural depravity, I was often concluding with the prophet that my strength and hope were perished from the Lord, and questioning why, if my experience was genuine, was it that I was now experiencing such vehement surgings of inward carnality and sin. I avoided the Lord's people, believing they regarded me as a hypocrite, and I was often harassed by the thought that I was a reprobate. At times I would get encouragement from portions of the Word of God. I also found the Memoirs of James Fraser of Brea helpful.[3] In one place he speaks of conviction of sin after conversion and quoted, and Oh! with what comfort to my distressed soul: 'But call to remembrance the former days, in which, after ye were illuminated, ye endured a great fight of afflictions' (Hebrews 10:32).

Shortly after this, the question of professing Christ publicly began to exercise me. I trembled at the thought of eating and drinking unworthily, and thereby eating and drinking damnation to myself. After a time, the way was made clear. Some days before the time came, I awoke one morning quoting these words, 'Take, eat: this is my body, which is broken for you.' On the Sabbath night after the Sacrament the enemy pursued my soul, smote my life down to the ground, and before his fiery assaults I felt myself helpless. On the Monday I was comforted and sweetly melted down by the words, 'Arise, shine; for thy light is come, and the glory of the LORD is risen upon thee.'

---

[3] James Fraser (1639–1699) was a Covenanter, who suffered repeated imprisonment for his principles. He was minister of Culross (Fife) from 1689. His autobiography was first published in 1738 as *Memoirs of the life of the very Reverend Mr. James Fraser of Brea: Minister of the Gospel at Culross.*

A year from the date of his conversion he got up early one morning and began to pray that the experience he had passed through at that time would be renewed. When he had prayed for some time, and given up all hope of obtaining his desire, the following words were applied to his soul, 'We have also a more sure word of prophecy; whereunto ye do well that ye take heed, as unto a light that shineth in a dark place, until the day dawn, and the day star arise in your hearts' (2 Peter 1:19). He was thus taught that the Word of God was to be his staff and his stay.

After his conversion, Mr MacLean became very exercised as to whether or not he should leave the Free Church and join the Free Presbyterian Church. Prior to his conversion he had been an ardent Free Churchman, and he and the present writer had many a lively though friendly debate on the respective positions of the two Churches. At that time neither of us was in a state of grace, but after his conversion it became a matter of great concern to him, and he was very much exercised in prayer over the matter. He also had to struggle with the ties of flesh and blood, for he had a very high regard for his father and a deep affection for his mother. He knew also that his brother and sisters would feel such a step, should he feel led to take it.

After some time, he came to the firm conclusion that the step should be taken. On the first occasion of his being in Lochcarron after he came to this mind, he had to pass the Free Church on his way to the Free Presbyterian Church. He felt the situation to be very trying, as his father was holding the service in the Free Church that particular

Sabbath morning. Having come to this mind, however, as a result of much exercise of soul, he did not waver.

He became a communicant in the Ness Congregation of the Free Presbyterian Church in 1935 as related above. Having become a Free Presbyterian in these circumstances, through much soul exercise, leading to a spiritual conviction as to the course of duty for him, he was loyally and affectionately attached to the testimony of our Church. This was very evident in his walk, life and witness. In this respect he was vastly different from many, whose lukewarmness with respect to the testimony for divine Truth in the Free Presbyterian Church is an eloquent demonstration of the fact that they are entire strangers to the spiritual experiences of Mr MacLean.

In the providence of God, he was not called up to the armed services during the Second World War. About this time, he became much exercised about another matter. Andrew Finlayson, the Missionary in Ness, had died, and Donald Thompson, the godly elder, was becoming old. Mr MacLean became exercised over his duty with respect to his beginning to take services in Ness. Eventually he felt led to do so, and having resigned his position as teacher in the Ness School, he became a Missionary in that congregation in 1941.

Some were of the opinion that he had enough light at this time to enter the ministry of the Church, but Mr MacLean did not at all share this opinion. He held very clear and definite views on the call to the ministry, and as he had fears, when he became a communicant, lest he should eat and drink damnation to himself, so he feared, above all things, to be one who would run without being sent, as a

Minister, in which event he would be a disaster to the Church, and make shipwreck of his profession. The solemn views he obtained, when brought to the knowledge of Christ, of man's fall, his inability to save himself, together with the sovereignty, holiness and glory of God, impressed upon him the solemn standing of professing to be an ambassador of Christ, dealing with the doctrines of God's Word and the eternal interests of souls. He therefore waited upon the Lord to call him, if that would be his holy will. He was much exercised over this, as he was in all spiritual matters. While praying earnestly over his case he was at a certain Communion. The table at which he sat was served by the late Rev. Donald Campbell, Edinburgh. Mr Campbell addressed the communicants from the words, 'My sheep hear my voice ... and they follow me.' He spoke of how the sheep of Christ heard the voice of the Lord in the law and then in the gospel. Mr MacLean felt he could follow the experiences of the sheep so far. Mr Campbell then went on rather unexpectedly to speak of Peter, and how he heard the voice of the Shepherd saying to him, 'Feed my sheep and feed my lambs.' Mr MacLean felt that as he had so closely followed the former part of the address, he could also respond to this call to be an under-shepherd to feed the flock of God. He applied to the Outer Isles Presbytery to be received as a student studying for the ministry of the Church, and was so received by that Court on 30th April 1946. He completed his divinity course under the Church tutors, who at that time were the Rev. Donald Beaton and the Rev. D.A. MacFarlane. On completion of his course he was licensed by the Outer Isles Presbytery in June 1948. A call being addressed to him by the Ness congregation, he accepted this, and was subsequently ordained and inducted to this congregation on 18th August of that year.

One of the attractive features of Mr MacLean's character was his affectionate disposition. On occasions this very trait may have led him to give a place to some who afterwards proved unworthy of it, but the fault was theirs and not his. Engaged in his ministry in the parish of Ness, in the exercise of a true and strong love to the souls of that congregation, the Lord was pleased to bless his labours to the ingathering of souls to Christ. On one occasion he wrote to a friend describing his experience the previous Sabbath evening in the little church at Skigersta. He had enjoyed remarkable liberty, and wrote that as he walked home he was convinced that 'every step I took was a step to eternal glory, and I felt such love to Ness that I could have kissed the ground'.

It therefore occasioned great surprise to his many friends, when, in 1962, he decided to accept a call to the congregation in Gisborne, New Zealand. Previous to this, he had been sent out by the Church as a Deputy to visit New Zealand and Australia. He had no idea then that his field of labour was to be changed. When the call came, however, he felt the Lord guiding him to leave the Ness he loved so much, and begin a ministry in Gisborne, on the other side of the world. The proof that he had the mind of the Lord in going was confirmed by the many seals to his ministry in these distant parts. His naturally ardent temperament, moulded by grace, made him ideal for the work of building up, not only the congregation in Gisborne, but also in Auckland. In both places he had the pleasure of seeing churches built and sizeable congregations formed, in which the doctrine, worship and government of the Reformed Church were established.

While minister in Gisborne, he often visited Australia, preaching in Sydney as well as in our congregation in Grafton, In all these places he was held in the highest regard, as a faithful preacher, a faithful and zealous minister of Christ, whose chief desire was the glory of God in the salvation of their souls. At a later stage, he was translated from Gisborne to Grafton, in Australia, and in 1976 returned home on being called to the Ness Congregation, where he was re-inducted on 10th February of that year.

As a preacher he was serious and solemn in his presentation of the Truth of God. Due to a tendency to speak rather quickly, he may not have been easy to follow on being heard for the first time, but this disadvantage would soon be overcome as his hearers became used to his manner of speaking. His doctrine was sound and scriptural as he set forth these great God-glorifying truths which he had so deeply learned in the experience of his own soul. His was not a formal ministry. He thirsted after the presence of God as he preached, and sought earnestly after the gracious liberty of the Holy Spirit, without which all is dark and barren. When this liberty was denied him, he became very cast down and mourned over his sad condition. On the other hand, as previously stated, when granted spiritual liberty, he greatly rejoiced, and thus truly experienced the meaning of the words of his Master, 'Take my yoke upon you and learn of me, for I am meek and lowly in heart; and ye shall find rest unto your souls.'

He was a clear preacher of law and gospel, and having many spiritual experiences himself he was able to meet the

Lord's people in their various experiences with a word of comfort and instruction. He was particularly helpful to them in handling their temptations, and showing the way in which the Lord was opening a door of escape from them. He was a true 'son of consolation'.

His preaching carried a strong note of witnessing, as he raised his voice against the moral and religious evils which abound in this evil and adulterous generation. This spirit of witness was also demonstrated in the many pamphlets which he wrote on such subjects as Arminianism, Mormonism, etc. These pamphlets were published by the Westminster Standard Publications, which was commenced by some of the young men in the Gisborne congregation who received spiritual benefit from his ministry. He wrote them under the pen name of Ergatees.[4]

As a man and a Christian, he was of a bright disposition, and an excellent companion to the spiritually minded. The eminently pious Miss Charlotte MacKay of Thurso used to say, 'I enjoy getting William MacLean's letters, they always seem to have good news.' Although no stranger to being cast down by reason of many temptations, he was a happy Christian. His mind dwelt very much on the Millennium, the beginnings of which he had hoped to see. He was consequently much in prayer for the conversion of the Jews, and spoke often of this on his deathbed.

It may not be out of place for the writer of this notice to remark that he and William MacLean were the closest of friends for over 50 years. On the last occasion that I assist-

---

[4] *Ergatees* is the Greek word for 'workman' in Matthew 10:10 and 2 Timothy 2:15.

ed him at the Ness Communion, when we came into the manse after the Sabbath morning service he asked me, 'When did we last sit together at the Lord's Table?' I replied that I could not remember. 'I do not think I shall sit at the Table again,' he said, 'for I felt so much of the presence of the Lord in the sermon and the Table address.' It was indeed the last time we sat together at the Lord's Table, though he himself did sit again the following March.

On 1st June 1985, he passed away to his everlasting rest, in his nephew's house in Stornoway. In his death the Lord's people have lost one who loved them and delighted in their company, as well as seeking their spiritual growth. Sinners have lost a faithful ambassador of Christ who prayed for them and sought the salvation of their souls. The Free Presbyterian Church has lost a gifted and zealous preacher of the everlasting gospel, who discerned the value of our testimony, and appreciated and loved our stand for the Word of God in its entirety. His many friends at home and abroad feel that a prince in Israel has indeed fallen. Their consolation is that they are assured that he is now among those of whom the Scripture says, 'Blessed are the dead which die in the Lord from henceforth: Yea, saith the Spirit, that they may rest from their labours; and their works do follow them' (Revelation 14:13). 'Help, LORD, for the godly man ceaseth; for the faithful fail from among the children of men' (Psalm 12:1).

REV. DONALD MACLEAN

God's covenant and baptism

Sermon before the baptism of two children

And I will establish my covenant between me and thee and thy seed after thee in their generations for an everlasting covenant, to be a God unto thee, and to thy seed after thee.

GENESIS 17:7

THE Lord in this chapter is establishing the covenant with Abram described in chapter 15. He gives him the seal of the covenant—the sacrament of circumcision—as an outward seal of the covenant.

The covenant of grace

At the beginning of the chapter, the Lord appears to Abram and says to him, 'I am the Almighty God; walk before me, and be thou perfect.' We believe there is a rebuke implicit in these words. In the preceding chapter we see how Abram on the advice of Sarai his wife, took Hagar, her Egyptian handmaid, to be his wife. They had come to the conclusion that, according to the course of nature, it was impossible for Sarai to have a son. She was past the age of childbearing. The Lord had promised a son to Abram, but the outlook looked unpromising, so they adopted this method in order to have the promise fulfilled. By Hagar, Abram had a son, Ishmael.

From the time of Ishmael's birth until he was thirteen or so, there was strife and dissension in Abram's household. What Abram did displeased the Lord: it was thirteen years after the birth of Ishmael that the Lord again appeared to him. He had been 86 years old when Ishmael was born (chapter 16:16), and he was 99 when the Lord appeared to him to establish the covenant. We cannot believe that these thirteen years were very happy years in the life of Abram. To all appearances the Lord did not appear or speak to him throughout these thirteen years, because of this false step that he took. Also in the strife and dissension that now entered his home—which before was a model of peace and of order—he could see the rod of the Lord upon him for what he had done.

But now, in his own time, thirteen years later, the Lord appears to Abram, and reveals himself as the Almighty God. He was in effect saying to Abram, 'Is there anything too hard for me?' 'Walk before me, and be thou perfect.' 'Be thou sincere. Walk before me in a consciousness of my almighty power, and not in the light of the sparks of your own kindling, setting limits to my power, and vainly trying to fulfil the promise in your own carnal way.' 'Is anything too hard for the LORD?' (Genesis 18:14). He can in his own appointed time fulfil his promise.

The Lord then goes on to establish his covenant. He also promises that Abram will have a son by Sarai, the promised seed. The Lord refers nine times to the covenant as *my* covenant', and on two occasions as the 'everlasting covenant'. This is the covenant which he had made with Abram, as it is recorded for us in chapter 15, a covenant sealed by the sacrifices which Abram offered. It is clear that this everlasting covenant, in which the Lord promises to be a God to him and to his seed after him, is the everlasting covenant of grace.

God was a God to Adam in a covenant of works, in a state of innocence. He promised to be a God to his seed. That covenant was based on the obedience that Adam would give, and on giving the obedience required according to the terms of the covenant Adam would be confirmed in a state of innocence. 'This do, and thou shalt live' (Luke 10:28).

But we see how Adam broke the covenant. He lost God for his portion. He lost the image of God and procured for himself and for his posterity the death threatened in the covenant. 'In the day that thou eatest thereof thou shalt surely die' (Genesis 2:17). On that day Adam died spiritually: he lost the Lord as his portion, the fountain of life and blessedness, and 'the god of this world' took possession of him. That is the condition into which Adam fell, and his posterity in him. 'The fall brought mankind into an estate of sin and misery.'

But the Lord revealed another covenant, which he had made in the eternal counsels before the foundation of the world: the everlasting covenant of grace, which he made with Christ, the eternally begotten Son, for all whom he purposed to save of the lost race to which we belong. This is the covenant of grace: it is from grace in God—

free and sovereign grace—that such a provision was made in the eternal counsels for the saving of lost and perishing sinners. Christ was set up as the Head and Mediator of that covenant, and all the election of grace—all whom God purposed to save—were given to him. As he himself says, 'Thine they were, and thou gavest them me.'

In the covenant Christ undertook to come and suffer and die in their stead, to restore that which he took not away and which Adam through his sin forfeited, to restore all the blessings. And that is what he did, in coming into this world and dying, the just in the room and stead of the unjust. He made reconciliation for iniquity and brought in everlasting righteousness. He procured eternal life for lost and perishing sinners, and God is now reconciled in Christ. That is the everlasting covenant of grace, and it was revealed to Adam in the first promise.

It is in that covenant of grace that God is offering and giving himself as God to sinners. That is the tenor of the covenant. He is not a God of salvation in the covenant of works but a righteous Judge, to execute the death threatened in the covenant. It is in the covenant of grace that he is revealed as a reconciled God in Christ. This is the covenant that the Lord made with Christ—the everlasting covenant of grace. In no other covenant does God offer himself to be a God to sinners, to be their portion in time and for eternity.

In Galatians chapter 3, verse 8, the covenant that the Lord made with Abram here is spoken of as the gospel. The apostle Paul (through the inspiration of the Holy Spirit) says that God 'preached before the gospel unto Abraham, saying, In thee shall all nations be blessed'. For the gospel is *the* good news: it sets forth the way of salvation, and the everlasting covenant of grace, devised in the eternal counsels of the Godhead, is the scheme of redemption. The way of salvation which Christ by his obedience unto death opened up is set before us in the gospel. It is the gospel which God preached to Adam and to Eve in the first promise, for Christ, who is the sum and substance of the gospel, was set before them as the seed of the woman who should bruise the head of the serpent.

It is the gospel that the Lord was preaching to Abram in making with him the everlasting covenant of grace, and in that covenant promising to be a God to him and to his seed—and not only to his seed according to the flesh (i.e. the Jewish people) but also all nations of the earth. 'In thy seed shall all nations of the earth be blessed' (Genesis 22:18). For the gospel is not for the Jews only but also for the Gentiles, and that blessing was revealed to Abram when the Lord established his covenant with him.

That is brought before us in verse 4 of our chapter: 'As for me, behold, my covenant is with thee, and thou shalt be a father of many nations.' The many nations, as the apostle Paul points out in Galatians 3, were the Gentiles who were to be brought in. The blessing of Abram was to come on the Gentiles through Jesus Christ. The Scriptures foresee that God would justify the heathen through faith. Abraham was to be the father of many nations—that is, of the heathen, Gentile nations.

This is the promise of the covenant: 'I will be a God unto thee and to thy people.' That is the sum and substance of all the blessings of the everlasting covenant of grace. If we have God as our portion—and we can only have him as

25

he is reconciled in Christ—then we have all the blessings. If Christ be yours, all things are yours. And we can only have God as he is revealed in Christ. 'No man cometh unto the Father, but by me' (John 14:6).

This is the blessing of the everlasting gospel which the covenant of grace brings before us. God is offering himself to us freely in Christ as a reconciled God. 'Incline your ear, and come unto me: hear, and your soul shall live; and I will make an everlasting covenant with you, even the sure mercies of David' (Isaiah 55:3).

The seal of the covenant

In establishing his covenant with Abram, the Lord gives the outward seal of circumcision. Abram and his household were to be circumcised. They were to have the seal of the covenant outwardly in their flesh. The Lord was thereby constituting as the visible church Abram and his seed, and the strangers who would sanctify themselves with Abram's household, receiving the truth that Abram had. They too would be brought into the visible church and be circumcised.

The Lord had a church in the world from the beginning. He effectually called Adam and Eve and set up the ordinances of his worship. But from the days of Abram till the coming of Christ, the visible church in this world was confined to Abram's seed, the people of Israel, the Jews. The door of admission into the visible church in Old Testament times was circumcision. Not only all who were born in Abram's household and in the household of his seed were to be circumcised on the eighth day, but also strangers who joined themselves to them, proselytes from the Gentiles. They too were to be circumcised. They were brought into the church through the door of circumcision. That was the 'middle wall of partition' between the church of God (his visible church) and those who were outside the pale of the visible church. They were uncircumcised, but all who were circumcised were within the pale of the visible church.

In our day baptism has taken the place of circumcision. It is the door of admission through which a person is publicly admitted into the visible church. Abram was a member of the visible church before he was circumcised. He believed the truths revealed to him by God. And it was on a profession of accepting these truths that persons were circumcised and received into the visible church. Likewise it is on a profession of faith that people receive baptism, for the visible church, as the Confession of Faith puts it, is 'made up of all who profess the true religion, and their children'.

'Who make a profession of the true religion.' That is, those who affirm their acceptance of the doctrines of the Bible. They believe the covenants. They believe that man by the fall lost God, and that the fall brought mankind into an estate of sin and misery, and that salvation is revealed in the everlasting covenant of grace. 'For by grace are ye saved through faith; and that not of yourselves: it is the gift of God: not of works, lest any man should boast' (Ephesians 2:8–9).

Just as in Old Testament times parents who were members of the visible church received circumcision for their children, so infants were received into the New Testament church, and this continues. It is the same covenant.

The covenant has not changed, although the seals have been changed with the coming of our Lord Jesus Christ. Instead of having the passover as one of the seals, pointing to the coming of the Saviour, we have in its place the Lord's Supper, commemorating his death. The paschal lamb pointed to the death that he *was* to die; now that he *has* died, there is no further need to observe the passover. In its place we have the sacrament of the Lord's Supper, the New Testament passover.

And in the place of circumcision we have baptism. The apostle Paul speaks of baptism as 'the circumcision of Christ' (Colossians 2:11–12). If infants were to be denied in the New Testament church the privileges they had had in the Old Testament church for about two thousand years, then a ruling would have been given, debarring children from enjoying the privileges which they enjoyed for twenty centuries in the Old Testament church.

The New Testament dispensation is a more liberal dispensation. It embraces not one nation but *all* the nations. And it would be very strange if, under the New Testament dispensation, children were to be deprived of a privilege they had had under the old dispensation. As most of the early converts to Christianity were Jews, they would naturally expect their children to belong to the visible church, and so receive baptism, the sacrament that took the place of circumcision. But there is not one syllable in the Bible which hints that infants should be debarred from receiving the privileges which they had had for twenty centuries. In fact, Christ says, 'Suffer little children to come unto me, and forbid them not: for of such is the kingdom of God' (Luke 18:16).

The phrase 'the kingdom of God' or 'the kingdom of heaven' in the New Testament means the visible church. That is clear from the parable where the kingdom of heaven is likened to ten virgins. Five were wise and five were foolish. Clearly 'the kingdom of heaven' there cannot refer to heaven itself, the kingdom of glory, for there are no foolish virgins in the kingdom of glory. It refers to the visible church in this world. Christ makes clear that infants have a right to this privilege in the visible church, because they belong to it.

The sacrament of circumcision was the door of admission into the church in Old Testament times. It was also a seal of the covenant. And what did circumcision seal? What was the Lord confirming by this seal? It was an outward seal pertaining to the visible church. The Lord was sealing his own promise, 'I will be a God unto thee and to thy seed.'

He was sealing the truth that righteousness—the righteousness of faith, the only righteousness which will stand us—is to be found in the covenant of grace. But an everlasting righteousness had to be wrought out by the head and mediator of the covenant, and that righteousness is freely offered to us in the gospel, and received by faith alone. That was what was sealed by circumcision.

Circumcision did *not* seal to a person that he had saving faith. It sealed that the Lord was promising or offering in the covenant that there was ample provision for the salvation of sinners in the covenant. We have the promise of the gospel. The gospel *is* a promise, for Christ is set forth and offered freely to sinners. That was sealed in Old Testament times in this outward way by circumcision, and in New Testament times by baptism.

Baptism does not seal that you have saving faith. Baptism is, as circumcision was, an outward ordinance pertaining to the visible church, and it seals, not an inward grace, but what the Lord reveals and offers freely in the covenant.

That is where Baptists [anti-paedobaptists] get confused with the sacrament of baptism. They fail to see the distinction between the visible church and the invisible church. The visible church is made up of all who profess the true religion. The invisible church is made up of all who are truly regenerate. 'The Lord knoweth them that are his' (2 Timothy 2:19). The seal of saving faith, where it is, is the Holy Spirit. They are sealed with the Holy Spirit unto the day of redemption (Ephesians 4:30). He is the seal of inward grace. The outward ordinance of baptism, which pertains to the visible church, is not a seal of saving faith but a seal of the covenant and of what the Lord is offering and freely promising in it.

To reiterate, where there is saving faith in the soul, the seal of that is the witness of the Holy Spirit. It is those who have saving faith and who are born again, who are sealed with the Holy Spirit. What baptism seals is the offer of the covenant. Christ is offered to us freely in the everlasting gospel and that offer is sealed in this outward way, that we receive the outward seal of the covenant in our being baptised. So, being baptised, we can plead before the Lord not only his own offer and promise, but also the seal that we have on us outwardly, the seal of the covenant. We can plead that the Lord would give us the inward seal, for the outward seal points to the necessity of the inward seal, the necessity of our being washed with the washing of regeneration and sealed by the Holy Spirit of promise, and the certainty that the Lord grants this grace to those who believe the promise.

The seed are included in the covenant

The fact that the covenant is the same covenant secures the continuity of the church across both the Old Testament and the New Testament. It is still the same church, but under a different dispensation.

Now, Baptists claim that the covenant the Lord made with Abram was a national covenant, and not the covenant of grace. It certainly had a national aspect, for the Lord promised in it to give Canaan to Abram's seed, but then Canaan was also a type of the heavenly Canaan. For we read of Abraham, Isaac and Jacob that they desired 'a better country', a country better than the ordinary Canaan, even 'an heavenly' (Hebrews 11:16).

Baptists not only deny that the covenant the Lord made with Abram was the covenant of grace, saying that it is a national covenant, but they deny also that baptism has taken the place of circumcision. They therefore break up the continuity of the church and bring in confusion. Baptism, in their opinion, is a seal of saving faith where it is; therefore, unless you can make a profession of saving faith then you will not be baptised. Whereas the baptism that seals saving faith is the baptism of the Holy Spirit in the soul. The inward seal of regeneration *is* the Holy Spirit. But baptism points to the need for regeneration.

That is clear from Galatians chapter 3. 'The scripture, foreseeing that God would justify the heathen through faith, preached before the gospel unto Abraham, saying, In thee shall all nations be blessed' (verse 8). 'For as many of you as have been baptised into Christ have put on Christ' (verse 27). 'And if ye be Christ's, then are ye Abraham's seed, and heirs according to the promise' (verse 29).

Now, these are not novel views that we hold in connection with baptism. These are the views held by the church of God in all ages and generations. 'Nothing on this has been more clearly demonstrated', writes Dr McCrie in his *Letters on Christian Baptism*, 'than that baptism of children was practised from the earliest ages of the church.'

Justin Martyr, born 100 AD, observes in his *Apologies*, when speaking of those who are members of the church, that part of these were sixty or seventy years old, who were made disciples of Christ from their infancy. But there was never any other mode of making disciples from infancy except baptism. He also writes of some who were known to himself and who were baptised as children within thirty-six years of the time Christ gave his commission to his disciples.

Origen, who was born about 185 AD of Christian parents, says it was the practice of the church to baptise infants and that this was in accordance with an order from the apostles.

Cyprian, who gives an account of the church of Carthage in 253 AD, says it was discussed in this venerable assembly whether infants were to be kept from baptism till they were eight days old, as in the case of circumcision, or might be baptised sooner. Without one dissenting voice the decree was returned that no infant was to be prohibited from the benefit of baptism even though only just born. Not the least objection appears to have been made about the lawfulness, the duty or propriety of baptising infants, but only about the precise time of the administration of baptism.

Augustine, born 354 AD, declares that the baptism of infants was the doctrine held by the church universal, and that not as instituted by church councils but delivered by the authority of the apostles alone. He says also that he did not remember meeting or reading any person, whether catholic [Christian] or heretic, who maintained that baptism ought to be denied to infants.

And Dr A.A. Hodge, in summing up his remarks on baptism in *Outlines of Theology*, says:

> The practice of infant baptism is an institution which exists as a fact and prevails throughout the universal church with the exception of the modern Baptists, whose origin can be definitely traced to the Anabaptists of Germany, about 1537. Such an institution must either have been handed down from the apostles or had a definite commencement as a novelty which must have been signalised by a decision and controversy. As a fact, however, we find it denoted in the very earliest records as a universal custom and as an apostolic tradition.

'Our argument is', says Dr Hodge, 'that infant baptism has prevailed: (a) from the apostolic age; (b) in all sections of the ancient church; (c) uninterruptedly till the present time; (d) in every one of the great historical churches of the Reformation. While its impugners or opposers date *since* the Reformation' (that is, from the time of the Anabaptists of 1537).

The Belgic Confession is very good on baptism. I will read an extract.

> Therefore, we believe that every man who is earnestly studious of obtaining life eternal ought to be but once baptized with this only baptism, without ever repeating the same: since we cannot be born twice. Neither does this baptism only avail us at the time when the water is poured upon us and received by us, but also through the whole course of our life. Therefore we detest the error of the Anabaptists, who are not content with the one only baptism they have once received, and moreover condemn the baptism of the infants of believers, who, we believe, ought to be baptized and sealed with the sign of the covenant, as the children in Israel formerly were circumcised upon the same promises which are made unto our children. And, indeed, Christ shed his blood no less for the washing of the children of the faithful than for adult persons; and, therefore, they ought to receive the sign and sacrament of that which Christ has done for them; as the Lord commanded in the law, that they should be made partakers of the sacrament of Christ's suffering and death shortly after they were born, by offering for them a lamb, which was a sacrament of Jesus Christ. Moreover, what circumcision was to the Jews, that baptism is to our children. And for this reason Paul calls baptism the circumcision of Christ.

The visible church is made up of all who profess, who believe the true gospel. Baptism is not a profession that they are in Christ, that they have saving faith. Baptism is an outward ordinance that pertains to them because they belong to the visible church. The Lord's Supper on the other hand is for persons who are his disciples in truth. It is a nourishing sacrament to nourish faith where it is, and it is therefore not for persons who are dead in trespasses and sins, but persons who have spiritual life. *That* sacrament—the Lord's Supper—is for the sustaining and upholding of spiritual life where it is.

This was the practice of church from New Testament times. And the apostles showed clear continuity with the church of Old Testament times. In Acts chapter 2, on the day of Pentecost, when the New Testament church was being established, we find Peter saying, as he calls on them to repent and be baptised, 'The promise is unto you and to your children, and to all that are afar off, even as many as the Lord our God shall call.' He is there quoting the very promise of the covenant which the Lord made with Abram. In that covenant the Lord said to Abram, 'In thee shall all nations of the earth be blessed.'

Administration of baptism

We shall now read our warrant for baptism. Baptism is a holy ordinance instituted by Christ, and we observe it in his church until he comes again. Just as with the Lord's Supper, the other sacrament of the New Testament, he gave the command, 'This do in remembrance of me; for as often as ye eat this bread, and drink this cup, ye do show forth the Lord's death till he come.'

Our warrant you will find in Matthew 28, from verse 18. 'And Jesus came and spake unto them, saying, All power is given unto me in heaven and in earth. Go ye therefore, and teach all nations, baptizing them in the name of the Father, and of the Son, and of the Holy Ghost: teaching them to observe all things whatsoever I have commanded you: and, lo, I am with you alway, even unto the end of the world. Amen.'

Now those who are bringing the children for baptism can come down to the front of the church.

Remarks before the administration of baptism

In this ordinance, the sacrament brings before us on the one hand that we are defiled on account of sin. We were born in sin and shapen in iniquity and we stand in need of being washed with the washing of regeneration. As Christ said to Nicodemus, 'Verily, verily, I say unto thee: except a man be born again, he cannot see the kingdom of God.' The water brings before us our need of washing, as we are defiled and polluted by sin.

The water also brings before us the provision that the Lord has made for the cleansing of sinners in the Son of his love. For Christ is the fountain opened for sin and for uncleanness, for the guilt of our state and the uncleanness of our nature. That was especially brought before Abram in the sacrament of circumcision: the need of being saved from the corruption of his nature.

Another truth is brought before us in this holy ordinance: our need of being justified—our need that our sins be blotted out—as well as our need of being delivered from the corruption of our nature. There is in Christ what can subdue our iniquities. Those who are regenerate have the promise that where he has begun a good work, he will continue it till the day of Jesus Christ. They will be delivered from the corruption of their nature.

It was said to the people in the temple, 'Thou shalt see greater abominations.' We believe that the longer believers live in the world, the deeper they are led to dig and to discover the abominations that are in their hearts. That makes them cry to the Lord for cleansing. Very often before a communion season, Satan can stir up these corruptions: 'Well, there you are, you've got all these corruptions in your heart, and you think you're a person who has undergone a saving change!' But that may be permitted so that the soul will cry to the Lord for cleansing, that he would subdue our iniquities and love us freely.

The water brings before us the fountain that is open and the invitation that is extended to sinners to come to Christ. 'Come now, and let us reason together, saith the LORD: though your sins be as scarlet. they shall be as white as snow; though they be red like crimson, they shall be as wool' (Isaiah 1:18).

The sprinkling of the water in the name of the Father, of the Son, and of the Holy Ghost, brings before us the application of the redemption purchased by Christ. The Holy Spirit applies that redemption to us in our effectual calling. It brings before us our need of the baptism of the Holy Spirit. We are not to be content with the outward ordinance: we are to seek the reality to which the outward ordinance points. This reality is the baptism of the Holy Spirit and his gracious and efficacious teaching.

Mephibosheth

Wednesday 29th March 1967
Prayer meeting address after Gisborne Communion season

And David said unto him, Fear not: for I will surely shew thee kindness for Jonathan thy father's sake, and will restore thee all the land of Saul thy father; and thou shalt eat bread at my table continually.

2 SAMUEL 9:7

IN the first part of the chapter we have an account of the enquiry that King David made. After he had been exalted to be king over all Israel, he made this enquiry: 'Is there not yet any of the house of Saul, that I may shew the kindness of God unto him?'

The house of Saul were David's sworn enemies; but now when David had the power and was king, instead of exercising that power in the way of taking vengeance on the house of Saul, he is here proclaiming that he is willing to show the kindness of God to any that are still left of the house of Saul.

He calls the kindness he was to show 'the kindness of God'. It is true of God that it is to his enemies that he shows lovingkindness, and David, by making this proclamation, was following the example of the Lord.

It was following this enquiry that Mephibosheth the son of Jonathan, Saul's grandson, was found in the house of Machir, the son of Ammiel, in Lodebar. David sent and fetched him from there. 'Now when Mephibosheth, the son of Jonathan, the son of Saul, was come unto David, he fell on his face, and did reverence.' From David's words to him, 'Fear not,' it would appear that Mephibosheth was afraid. His fear no doubt was that he would be cut off because he belonged to the house of Saul, David's sworn enemies.

But when making reverence before the king, David addressed him by name: 'Mephibosheth.' There was kindness and love in that one word, the way in which he spoke to him. Mephibosheth said, 'Behold thy servant!' David's gracious and magnanimous answer is in the words of our text.

In seeking to make a spiritual use of this incident, we may take Mephibosheth to typify the sinner whom the Lord seeks out and brings nigh to himself, the sinner that he brings from the Lodebar of a state of nature to be at his own table. Lodebar was far off from Jerusalem, but Mephibosheth was found there in the house of Machir and brought to the king's table. And that is true of all sinners whom the Lord brings nigh to himself: he finds them in the Lodebar of a state of nature and brings them nigh to himself. He seeks them out, as we were singing in the Psalm: 'Bless'd is the man whom thou dost chuse, / and mak'st approach to thee, / that he within thy courts, O Lord, / may still a dweller be' (Psalm 65:4).

1. So, in the first place, we may take Mephibosheth as typifying the sinner whom the Lord seeks out and brings to himself.

2. And in the second place, we may make a few remarks on the kindness of the Lord. David, in seeking for any who were left of the house of Saul, said that he was to show them the kindness of God; and the kindness of God is revealed in drawing sinners to himself.

3. In the third place we shall consider the promise that belongs to all the sinners sought out by the Lord: 'Fear not: for I will surely shew thee kindness', etc.

1. Mephibosheth, typifying the unregenerate person

We read concerning Mephibosheth that he was lame in both his feet. When he was a little child, and his nurse was fleeing with him in her arms on hearing of the deaths of Saul and Jonathan, in her haste she dropped Mephibosheth, and as a result of that fall he was lame on both his feet.

A person who is lame on both his feet is in a miserable condition. It is as a result of the fall that all mankind are in an estate of sin and misery. All the miseries of this world and all the miseries of hell are a result of the fall, for the fall exposed us to all the miseries of this life, to death itself, and to the pains of hell forever.

There are two respects in which sinners are spiritually lame. First, they have no standing before God. In a state of innocence Adam had a standing before God: he was created with a holy nature, and he was therefore able in thought, word and deed to give to the law that perfect obedience which the law required. He was able to give to the law a righteousness commensurate with its demands. But, through the Fall, Adam lost that ability. He lost the image of God, and instead of being holy in his nature, he had a nature that was altogether defiled and corrupt; a sinful nature. And on that account he could not give to the law the obedience it requires; not even to the extent of one holy thought; for 'who can bring a clean thing out of an unclean? No one.'

The sinner in a state of nature therefore has no standing before God. Any standing he may think he has is but a foundation of sand. If we are to have a standing before God it is not in our own righteousness, but in the right-eousness of the Lord from heaven. It is in Christ we can have a standing: in ourselves we are in a state of condem-nation. In Christ we can be accepted and be reconciled to God, and have a standing before the Judge of all the earth. This was true of Daniel: we find the Lord saying to him, 'Go thou thy way till the end be: for thou shalt rest, and stand in thy lot at the end of the days' (Daniel 12:13).

Rest awaits those who are found in Christ, 'accepted in the Beloved', and whose hope and faith is nothing less than Jesus' blood and righteousness. Daniel may have been cast down and faint because of the way, as the Lord's own people oftentimes are, but this promise was given him, that rest awaited him, and at the great day of judg-ment he would have a standing place at the right hand of the Judge. It is in Christ we can have a standing place: we have no standing of our own. It is a result of the fall that we are lame in that respect.

But we are lame also in a second respect, that we are totally unable to love the Lord and to give to the law that obedience which the law requires. Our inability is a proof of the state of condemnation and alienation in which we are. We are still responsible for our sins and for the condition into which our sins have brought us. A person may be in debt and quite unable to pay the debt, but the law of the land still holds him responsible—his creditors will still hold him responsible for his debt—and he can be summoned to court and charged. His want of ability to pay his debts will not excuse him.

Similarly, we are responsible, and God will hold us responsible for our sins. They are *our* sins, the sins which *we* have committed—and for them God shall hold us answerable. The only hope for us is that we will cry to him for mercy, for he has revealed himself as a sin-pardoning God in Christ. 'Who is a God like unto thee, that pardoneth iniquity, and passeth by the transgression of the remnant of his heritage? he retaineth not his anger for ever, because he delighteth in mercy' (Micah 7:18).

We note that Mephibosheth belonged to the family of Saul, who proved himself such a bitter enemy of David. It is true of us spiritually that we are enemies in our minds by wicked works, and of the family of Satan. As Christ said to others, 'Ye are of your father the devil, and the lusts of your father ye will do' (John 8:44). This is the condition of sinners.

Mephibosheth was in the house of Machir in Lodebar, far off from Jerusalem, far off from the king's table and the king's palace. The name 'Machir' means 'one that sells'. Spiritually we are far off from the king's table and we may think of Satan, the one that sells what will satisfy and gratify the lusts of sinners. In the *Pilgrim's Progress* we read about Vanity Fair. In Vanity Fair all manner of wares were sold, and if you did not find what you wanted in one street of the fair, you could be directed to some other street.

You could buy anything at Vanity Fair: there was only one thing you could not buy, and that was the Truth. When Christian and Faithful passed through the fair, they were called upon and urged to buy the wares on display. They answered, 'We buy the Truth.' The Truth was not to be found there, but all kinds of merchandise that would destroy sinners for eternity.

That is true in our day: the world is just one great Vanity Fair. People are given over to the vanities of this world. The Lord says, 'My son, give me thine heart,' and the sinner says, 'No, I'll give my heart to Satan. He'll give me what will gratify and satisfy me.' Not only is that true of the vain world, but the churches of our day are to a large extent places of merchandise instead of being houses of prayer. The churches of our day have become part of Vanity Fair. Places where the Truth was formerly proclaimed are turned into houses of merchandise and vanity. In fact, dances are held under the auspices of some churches, and instead of reproof you will find deadly arrows. God shall shoot at them with an arrow (Psalm 64:7).

The house of Machir was in Lodebar. 'Lodebar' means 'a place without pasture', a desert, barren place. That is what the world will become to all who are called by grace. They will not find what will feed their souls in the Lodebar of this world. Maybe Mephibosheth was quite at home in the house of Machir and in Lodebar, with the merchandise that Machir had. He was in a place where there was no pasture. That is true of those who are not of Christ's sheep, who are not following him and seeking to be led into the green pastures of his Truth. The unregenerate are content with a form of godliness, but ignorant of the power thereof.

2. The kindness of David, typifying the kindness of God

In the second place, we come to notice a few things about the kindness of David as typifying the kindness of God.

It was following David's proclamation that Mephibosheth was found in the house of Machir in Lodebar. We see that the kindness of David was 'for Jonathan's sake'. It was for Jonathan's sake that Mephibosheth was brought from Lodebar to eat bread continually as one of the king's sons at the king's table. We see how dear Jonathan and David were to one another. Jonathan loved David 'as his own soul' (1 Samuel 18:1) and David said of Jonathan's love, 'Thy love to me was wonderful, passing the love of women' (2 Samuel 1:26).

The love between Jonathan and David found expression in the making of a covenant between them. David promised that he would not cut off Jonathan's family; that he would spare them and uphold them. Spiritually, it is from the fathomless ocean of the love of a triune God that sinners, lost and ruined and hell-deserving, are brought nigh. As we read: 'Yea, I have loved thee with an everlasting love: therefore with lovingkindness have I drawn thee' (Jeremiah 51:3). And that love, which flows out to a number that no man can number of sinners in the Lodebar of a state of nature, slaves to sin and to Satan, found expression in the making of a covenant. God the Father entered into a covenant with God the Son, and Christ undertook in the everlasting covenant of grace to work out eternal redemption for all who were given to him.

The kindness of God is seen in the making of the covenant of grace, in his not leaving the whole human race to perish. His kindness is seen when, according to the good pleasure of his will, he elected some to everlasting life, and entered into a covenant of life with Christ as their Redeemer. His lovingkindness is seen in his sending his only begotten Son into this world. 'Herein is love, not that we loved God, but that he loved us, and sent his Son to be the propitiation for our sins' (1 John 4:10).

In his human nature Christ wrought out an everlasting righteousness, made an atonement for sin, and is now exalted to be a Prince and a Saviour for to give repentance and remission of sins unto Israel.

The lovingkindness of the Lord is to be seen in the gospel offer. The proclamation of lovingkindness that David made was to his enemies, persons who belonged to the family of Saul. So it is with the gospel offer. 'Thou hast, O Lord, most glorious, / ascended up on high; / and in triumph victorious led / captive captivity: / Thou hast received gifts for men, / for such as did rebel; / yea, ev'n for them, that God the Lord / in midst of them might dwell.' (Psalm 68:18).

It is to sinful, hell-deserving rebels that the gospel is to be preached. Some think that the gospel is to be preached only to those who are under concern. But the effect of that is to keep the poor sinner examining himself to see if he's got true concern. If he believes that the offer is based on the concern which he has, or on the repentance which he can produce, that poor sinner will spend his time trying to make himself concerned and wondering if he's truly concerned, or truly penitent, before he will think of looking to Christ and the warrant that he has for believing in Christ as he is freely offered to him in the gospel.

Christ is not offered to you on account of any concern you may have. He is not offered to you on the grounds of any repentance you may think you have. He is offered to you just as you are, lost, ruined and hell-deserving, for out of Christ you can have no true repentance. You can have nothing out of Christ. 'O Israel, thou hast destroyed thyself; but in me in thine help' (Hosea 13:9). All help, and all salvation, is to be found in him alone, and the offer comes to you in the gospel just as you are. He sent the gospel to 'every creature'. Christ is set before you in all his fulness as a Saviour. You are confronted at this moment with Christ and the everlasting blessings that are treasured up in him, or the merchandise that you will find in Vanity Fair.

All that Satan, the god of this world, can give you, is material things. Your choice is Christ or the world; Christ or Belial; Christ or Barabbas. You shall be held responsible for how you deal with the offer of Christ in the gospel.

It was through this proclamation of lovingkindness that Mephibosheth was found, far away in Lodebar. Christ in the gospel will seek out every Mephibosheth whom he has purposed to save. Then Lodebar will become a place without pasture to that sinner: he cannot be at home any longer in Machir's house. He finds himself afar off in

Lodebar, 'without God and without hope in the world', as the prodigal son did in the far country. He had been in his element, abandoning himself to riotous living in the midst of Vanity Fair, but a day came in the history of the prodigal son when famine came into his soul, and he discovered that there was nothing in the far country that could meet the needs of his soul. The far country became to him a place without pasture, Lodebar.

It is a hopeful sign when sinners lose their taste for the vanities in which they used to find pleasure and satisfaction, when they had no word of being at the King's table. They are now seeing 'vanity of vanities' written above all that Lodebar can give them.

There is a drawing power in the everlasting gospel. Christ says: 'And I, if I be lifted up from the earth, will draw all men unto me' (John 12:32). There is a secret drawing of the soul to the New Testament David, although the sinner may be trembling for fear that because of his sins—because he belongs to the family of Saul—he is to be cut off, that God is going to come forth in judgment to cut him off.

3. The promise to Mephibosheth

Mephibosheth was brought before David. He was now face to face with the king, and he fell prostrate and 'did reverence'. It is clear from our text that he was afraid. But David said, 'Mephibosheth.' There was lovingkindness in that one word. When David addressed him by name, what an uplift of soul he must have felt! He could see by the loving way in which David spoke to him, that there was kindness in the heart of the king toward him, and not wrath.

The sinner is brought to prostrate himself before the Lord, to wait on the Lord, and to receive from the Lord what gives him a hope. He gets that through the Word of God. The way David spoke to Mephibosheth kindled a hope in his soul that all was to be well with him, that he was not to be cut off. He had been afraid, but David's words 'Fear not', etc., dispelled all that dread of death and of punishment. One word, or one verse, may dispel the slavish fear from the soul of a sinner and cause his soul to go forth in confidence and in trust to the Saviour. Mephibosheth was able to trust David as one who was to spare his life and show mercy to him. The king's words brought peace to his soul.

In this promise, David opens up to Mephibosheth why he was brought nigh; why he was brought from the house of Machir in Lodebar. It was 'for Jonathan's sake' and for the sake of the covenant that was between David and Jonathan. Now, those who are brought nigh have no desire to return to the place from whence they came. 'And truly, if they had been mindful of that country from whence they came out, they might have had opportunity to have returned. But now they desire a better country, that is, an heavenly; wherefore God is not ashamed to be called their God: for he hath prepared for them a city' (Hebrews 11:15–16). They are now seeking to be fed from the table of the gospel, from the table of the New Testament David. They do not desire to go back to feed upon the vanities and the pleasures of sin which they had at one time in the house of Machir in Lodebar. The time past of their life sufficeth them to have been living in diverse lusts and pleasures.

Their confession is: 'Of iniquity / too long we have the workers been; / we have done wickedly' (Psalm 106:6). They are seeking to be receiving from the gospel table. Christ has become precious to them, and they seek to be in him, and for him, in the world.

Mephibosheth had fears. And those who have a hope that they have been brought nigh to the Lord and accepted in the Beloved will have fears. They will have a sense of their own unworthiness. We see how unworthy Mephibosheth felt himself to be in the light of all the kindness that David was promising to show him. 'He bowed himself, and said, What is thy servant, that thou shouldest look upon such a dead dog as I am?' This will be true of the Lord's own people: they will have a sense of the spiritual death they find within; of their corruptions and lameness; their inability to run as they would desire in the way of God's commandments. These things cause them to have fears as to whether they are of the Lord's true people or not.

The Lord is able to speak a word in season to those who are weary in connection with their fears. It is said that there are 365 'Fear nots' in the Bible. That shows how many and how varied are the fears of the Lord's people, that they need this encouragement from the Lord himself when cast down under a sense of their own unworthiness. How lame and backward they find themselves! They are lame on both their feet. As someone put it,—I think it was Archibald Cook—they are lame on their calling and they are lame on their election.

That is one of their fears: have they been truly called? Is it a true work of grace that has been wrought in their souls? Or are they just but foolish virgins, having a name to live and a lamp of profession, and only deceiving themselves? It is true of many of the Lord's people that they are lame on their calling and election. If they could make their calling sure, they would be sure of their election. And they are called upon to make their calling sure—to make sure that they are in Christ—to make sure that they have been called effectually. And if they make their calling sure, they then shall be sure of their election. But many of them find themselves lame on their calling and lame on their election.

It is true that the Lord gives assurance, and that is what they seek after—an assurance of their interest in Christ. But the fact that they are exhorted to make their calling and election sure shows that they can be called effectually and justified freely, and yet not be sure that that is true concerning them. The sinner may entertain a hope, and be encouraged in his hope, and yet at times feel as if his hope has just perished from the Lord. But all who are called effectually are justified, and shall be at last glorified—and it is true of them that they seek to be fed from the table of the gospel. The Lord is in covenant with all whom he has brought nigh, and all these 'Fear nots' are the promises of the covenant, all of which are yea and amen in Christ Jesus.

'For Jonathan thy father's sake.' It is for Christ's sake that they are blessed, and it is for Christ's sake that they seek all the blessings of which they desire to be partakers. Not for their own sakes, for they are conscious of their own unworthiness. There is this in the covenant for them, that all they lost in the fall through their father Adam is restored to them in Christ. The image that they lost through the fall shall be restored in its fulness to their souls at death, for 'he which hath begun a good work in you will perform it until the day of Jesus Christ' (Philippians 1:6). Their souls at death shall be made perfect in holiness, and their bodies at the resurrection made like unto Christ's glorious body. They shall be 'heirs of God, and joint-heirs with Christ' (Romans 8:17). All that they lost in Adam is restored in the last Adam, the Lord from heaven.

Christ himself declares that he restored that which he took not away. He restored it as a surety and substitute for his people. David here reveals to Mephibosheth the blessings of the covenant that was between himself and Jonathan: it was for Jonathan's sake that Mephibosheth was receiving all these blessings, and all that he had lost was to be restored to him. He was to eat bread at the king's table continually as one of the king's sons. And the Lord reveals to those who have a hope that they were brought nigh, a Word on which to build their hope for eternity. They got peace through the gospel, and encouragement to commit their souls to Christ alone—to look to him. Their sense of their own deadness and corruption does not cut them off from the covenant or from the blessings of the covenant.

The covenant of works was in the keeping of Adam, but Adam fell and broke the covenant. But the keeping of the covenant of grace is not in the hands of his people. Although the Lord is in covenant with them, the keeping of the covenant is in the hands of the covenant head—in the hands of Christ their Mediator. Therefore it is a covenant that is ordered in all things and sure, a covenant that shall never break. As he declares, 'The mountains shall depart, and the hills be removed; but my kindness shall not depart from thee, neither shall the covenant of my peace be removed, saith the LORD that hath mercy on thee' (Isaiah 54:10).

What a consolation is there for the heirs of promise! With their sense of their own unworthiness and deadness, finding themselves no better than a dead dog, unworthy of anything from the hand of the Lord, so lame on both their feet! To them the Lord says, 'Fear not. I will restore thee all that thou hast lost. All the blessings that you are given are for Christ's sake.' Mephibosheth's sense of his own unworthiness was not to keep him from sitting at the king's table as one of the king's sons, for David was looking on him in the light of the love and in the light of the covenant that was between himself and Jonathan.

And the Lord looks on his people in Christ, and not as they are in themselves. They are called therefore to look to the one who *is* worthy. That is their own prayer and desire: 'O let thy hand be still upon / the Man of thy right hand, / the Son of man, whom for thyself / thou madest strong to stand' (Psalm 80:17).

The prayer of the child of God is that the Lord would not look upon him as he is in himself, but that he would look upon him in the face of his 'anointed dear'. In him the Father sees no iniquity in Jacob, neither hath he seen perverseness in Israel (Numbers 23:21). This is the assurance that the New Testament David gives his Mephibosheths, although they perceive themselves as so unlike any of the king's sons or daughters. This is in the covenant: 'For *Christ's* sake you shall eat bread at my table continually.'

Guests may be invited to the table of a king or queen, and they are honoured. Then they go away and that is the end of the matter: they may never sit at the royal table again. But the Lord promises his people that they will be eating bread *continually* at the table of the gospel. He will provide for their needs as long as they are in this world. Although in their own estimation they are no better than a dead dog, they have a warrant to sit at the table he has provided for them in the wilderness. Their sense of unworthiness may be a temptation to them after a communion season, after they have kept their vows. But the Lord says to them, 'You shall eat at my table, as one of the king's sons.'

There was a day in Mephibosheth's life when he never thought he would be at the king's table. Such a thought never entered his mind. There are many at the Lord's Table who, a few years ago, had no thought of professing the Lord or witnessing on his side. It was as distant from their minds as east is from the west. Yet the Lord sought them out and brought them to his table. And we should be seeking, when we hear the gospel preached, that the Lord would seek us out and bring us to himself, that he would fit us and make us Mephibosheths, and that he would save us by his grace.

We will be conscious of our own lameness, and the power of our own infirmities, our own deadness, and our need that the Lord would give us from the gospel table what would quicken and sustain us. We shall become debtors all our days to free and sovereign grace. The Lord does not give his people a stock of grace, as it were. Adam had a stock of grace in himself but he fell. But the Lord in 'times convenient / bestows on them their food'. They

54

are kept a poor and needy people—otherwise they would become self-sufficient. The Most High pours them from vessel to vessel, that they may be dependent on himself, and learn what all his disciples learn: 'Without me, ye can do nothing' (John 15:5).

What a blessing if we were all brought to this! We should be seeking that the Lord will not leave us, and praying that he would remember us. We should be praying: 'Remember me, Lord, with that love / which thou to thine dost bear; / with thy salvation, O my God, / to visit me draw near: / that I thy chosen's good may see, / and in their joy rejoice; / and may with thine inheritance / triumph with cheerful voice' (Psalm 106:4–5).

Oh, that this would be the desire of our souls, that the Lord would draw us and prepare us; that we would leave the house of Machir and turn our backs on every Lodebar of this world; and that we would be found at his table, witnesses on his side in our day and generation! You may have been envying the Lord's people at the table here on Sabbath, and saying, 'It would be good to be of them, to be truly one of his people.' Well, that is something you should cherish. And if that is the sincere desire of your soul, it will be leading you, as it led the Greeks, away from the country where they were, to worship the Lord at Jerusalem. It will lead you to seek and to follow the Lord. 'Delight thyself in God; he'll give / thine heart's desire to thee. / Thy way to God commit, him trust, / it bring to pass shall he. / And, like unto the light, he shall / thy righteousness display; / and he thy judgment shall bring forth / like noon-tide of the day' (Psalm 57:4–6).

What a blessing it would be, to be found among those who are at the King's table in truth, dependent upon him to receive what would meet the needs of our souls! And Christ is able to do that for us. He makes known his power to save, and his willingness to save, in the everlasting gospel. Many a Mephibosheth he has sought out, who for many a long year had no thought that they would ever be followers of Christ in this world.

He is still the same, and what he did for others he is able to do for you. You be casting yourself at his feet and crying to him that he would form you and fashion you for himself; that you would not be left in the house of Machir in Lodebar, in a place where there is no pasture, but that you would be found among his sheep and his lambs. All who are Christ's sheep and Christ's lambs seek to follow the Good Shepherd and to be led into the green pastures of his Truth.

May he bless his Truth.

Naaman's confession

Lord's Day, 20th December 1964

Behold, now I know that there is no God in all the earth, but in Israel.

2 KINGS 5:15

WE have in these words the confession that Naaman the Syrian made to Elisha the prophet after he had been miraculously cured of his leprosy. Not only was he miraculously cured in his body, but we believe that in connection with this miracle he came to a saving knowledge of the God of Israel.

1. In the first place we may make a few remarks on the God of Israel.

2. Secondly, the way in which Naaman the Syrian, a man who was an idolater and a stranger to the commonwealth of Israel, an uncircumcised Gentile, was brought to a knowledge of the God of Israel.

3. Thirdly the proofs that he gave that his knowledge was saving. To know the God of Israel is life eternal.

1. The God of Israel

A few remarks in the first place on the God of Israel, that is, the one living and true God. 'For all the gods are idols dumb, / which blinded nations fear; / but our God is the Lord, by whom / the heav'ns created were' (Psalm 96:5).

We read, 'O Israel: The LORD our God is one LORD.' In Hebrew the word translated 'one' means 'a unity'. The God of Israel is a unity. Implied in these words is the mystery of the Trinity, the three persons in the one Godhead. By the Godhead we understand the essence or the nature. In the divine nature there are three persons: the Father, the Son and the Holy Ghost; and these three are one God, the same in substance, equal in power and glory.

That is the mystery of the Trinity. There are three persons eternally subsisting in the Godhead, in the divine nature. Each of them has the fulness of the divine nature and all its attributes. We speak of the Father as the first person, the Son as the second person, and the Holy Spirit as the third person, but these designations do not imply any preference or inequality. It is a mere order. They are revealed in that order, but there are no degrees in the Godhead. They are all equal in power and in glory, and the fulness of the Godhead belongs to each of the divine persons.

That is the mystery of the Trinity. It is the will of God that in every age and generation, believers should be taught concerning the God of Israel, that he is a unity. He who denies this mystery proves that he is a stranger to grace and to God. Every person who denies the doctrine of the Trinity is going to hell. If we deny this basic and fundamental doctrine, we show clearly that we do not belong to his people, the Israel of God.

The Word of God also brings before us the personal properties peculiar to each of the persons, the eternal relationships in which they stand one to another. That too is a divine mystery. It is the personal property of the Father to beget the Son, and that from all eternity; and it is the personal property of the Son to be eternally begotten of the Father; and it is the personal property of the Holy Spirit to eternally proceed from the Father and from the Son.

Our finite understandings cannot encompass the mysteries pertaining to the eternal God. He is called 'the God of Israel' because in Old Testament times all the revelation that the eternal God gave of himself was confined to Israel. The revelation he gave of himself as Creator, Lawgiver, Judge and Saviour—all these divine revelations were confined to one nation, the people of Israel. And all these revelations that God gave of himself are in and through Christ. The Lord Jesus Christ is the sum and substance of all these revelations. 'No man hath seen God at any time; the only begotten Son, which is in the bosom of the Father, he hath declared him' (John 1:18).

The God of Israel is spoken of as the God of truth. He is to be found in his own Word. Christ describes the Old Testament Scriptures thus: 'The word of God that cannot be broken.' The same can be said of the Scriptures of the New Testament. It is in the volume of the book, from Genesis to Revelation, that we can come to a saving knowledge of the God of Israel, the God of truth. Any conception of God that is not based upon the Scriptures is a false conception.

The God of Israel is especially brought before us as the God of salvation. In Christ he is a reconciled God; out of Christ he is a consuming fire. In Christ he reconciles sinners to himself. As the Saviour declares, 'I am the way, the truth, and the life: no man cometh unto the Father, but by me' (John 14:6).

The God of Israel was set before the people of Israel as the God of salvation in the glory of Christ's person and the work he was to finish. That was kept before them in the promises and in the sacrifices, and in all the types of the Old Testament church. 'He of salvation is the God, / who is our God most strong; / and unto God the Lord from death / the issues do belong' (Psalm 68:20). He is the one to whom we must render our account, and he requires of us as his creatures that we would worship him in spirit and in truth.

To come to know the God of Israel as he is revealed in Christ, that is life eternal. 'This is life eternal, that they might know thee the only true God, and Jesus Christ, whom thou hast sent' (John 17:3). We can never come to a knowledge of God—that is, a saving knowledge of God—but as he is revealed in Christ. Philosophy and science can never give us this saving knowledge of the Lord. We need the teaching of the Holy Spirit to impart spiritual life to our souls. And if we have spiritual life, as we believe Naaman received for his soul in connection with this miracle, then we too shall give proofs that we have spiritual life in our souls.

2. How Naaman was brought to saving knowledge

We shall notice in the second place how Naaman was led to a saving knowledge of the Lord.

In Old Testament times the revelations which God gave of himself were confined to one nation—to the people of Israel. But there were among the Gentiles those who were brought in, such as Ruth the Moabitess and Rahab the harlot and Naaman here. These were indeed heirs of Zion, although the Lord was yet to bring in the Gentiles. The middle wall of partition between Jew and Gentile was yet to be broken down. That was done through the death of Christ, and millions of the Gentiles have since been gathered in. In Naaman's time only very few were being brought in, but when God's appointed time came, the Gospel was sent to the Gentiles and multitudes have been gathered in to a saving knowledge of the God of Israel. The Jews—the chosen people—who had these revelations rejected the Saviour, and for nearly two thousand years they have been blinded. A veil of delusion is upon that people. But when the Lord's time comes, they too shall be gathered in.

In this chapter is described the remarkable way in which the Lord brought Naaman to a knowledge of himself. 'God moves in a mysterious way, his wonders to perform.' In the ruling of his providence there are wheels within wheels.

First we have the young maid of the land of Israel who was taken captive by the Syrians. She was a maid in Naaman's household. That was a very sore and sad providence for her parents and for herself. No doubt they were just dumb with grief. This young maid was snatched away from her home and was taken to a foreign land, and was a slave there in Naaman's household. But the hand of the Lord was to be seen in her circumstances: the Lord had need of her. To that land she had to go.

Then Naaman developed leprosy, a deadly disease. Had not the Lord intervened, it would have brought him to death. He was a great man, captain of the host of the king of Syria, 'a great man with his master, and honourable, because by him the LORD had given deliverance unto Syria: he was also a mighty man in valour. But he was a leper' (verse 1). Although he had all these honours and was held in such high esteem by the king, and had earned such a name for himself as a valiant commander, this was spoiling all that he had: he had a terminal disease.

Then one day this maid said to her mistress, Naaman's wife, 'Would God my lord were with the prophet that is in Samaria! for he would recover him of his leprosy.' She remembered the prophet Elisha and no doubt had heard of the miracles that he was enabled to do. So she tells her mistress of him. Naturally Naaman would avail himself of every means that he would hear of, in order that he might be cured of his deadly disease. If there was a cure in the land of Israel, he was determined that he would make trial of it.

So, he brings the matter before the king. And as he was a friend of the king of high standing, the king drafted a letter and gave it to Naaman. Then, with his retinue and with handsome presents—ten talents of silver and six thousand pieces of gold, and ten changes of raiment—Naaman set off for the land of Israel and made for the palace of the king. The king of Syria out of courtesy had addressed the letter to the king of Israel. He would not have his commander-in-chief entering the land of Israel privately, as it were: he might be taken for a spy. It would have been anything but courteous for him to enter the land without making contact, considering his position and considering that he was being sent by the king.

So the letter was presented to the king of Israel. As far as one can judge from the account, it appears unlikely that Naaman entered the palace. The king's reaction of mixed alarm and suspicion is recorded in the seventh verse of our chapter. He must have made these observations to his courtiers in the palace. If Naaman had been present when the letter was read, he would have given the necessary explanation. The king of Israel's conclusion was that this was but a pretext to declare war on him by seeking a quarrel against him, when no such thoughts were in the mind of the king of Syria.

We can see why the king came to this conclusion. The Syrians had gone out by companies, and had brought away many like the little maid captive out of the land of Israel. Before now Israel had been harassed by the Syrians. These past events would have left their impression on the king's mind, and with this background of the losses re-cently sustained and the captives taken, the letter seemed a new excuse for invading the land and making war. He was so convinced of this conclusion that he rent his clothes. There was no doubt in his mind about the matter. In fact, the king of Syria was quite innocent of any such intention. How often we have discovered in our own experience, how we can come to conclusions from, per-haps, a word spoken or some action! In the light of these impressions, we interpret actions and situations according to our own minds, and can come to conclusions which are far from being just. The king of Syria thought that the king of Israel would readily comprehend the whole matter from the facts that he gave; if there were any omissions, Naaman could give the necessary explanations.

The king had only part of the story. If he had sent word out to Naaman and enquired further instead of complaining querulously to his courtiers, he would have got all the facts, and that would have put a different light on the matter altogether. He would have seen how mistaken his conclusion was. But so sure was he of it that he rent his clothes. He was enraged at the idea that the king of Syria was seeking a quarrel.

When we jump to conclusions in the light of 'facts'—I speak from my own experience—and we find our emotions stirred up; when anger is aroused and we determine that we will take such-and-such a course of action, we can be almost certain that Satan has a hand in the matter. It becomes us to take time and wait until we have all the facts in our possession before we act. Although the facts before us may be very convincing, and we may be interpreting them according to the disposition of our own minds, just as the king of Israel did here, we may, like him, be totally unjust in our conclusions. Consider the wrong he did an innocent person: the king of Syria was entirely innocent of seeking a quarrel at this time. When we come to rash conclusions, we are prone to act precipitately and not with due care and prayer. What harm we may do to persons who are wholly innocent! Most of us know this from our own experience.

The prophet Elisha heard that the king had rent his clothes. No doubt this news spread like wildfire. The king must have thought that the Syrians were at that moment mustering on his borders—there would be a raid at any moment—and as the rumour was spread, the blacker the rumour would get. But there was not a particle of truth in it! It was merely a fabrication, a mesh of distorted facts and wrong conclusions. As a godly man once said, 'You could see the hand of Satan behind it all,' for Satan was determined that he would come between Naaman and his interview with the prophet of the Lord. The heathen nations were under the power of Satan, and Satan was afraid that if Naaman came into contact with God's prophet and with the Truth of the Lord, it might be blessed to his soul, and he might be plucked as a brand from the burning. Therefore we see Satan putting all his irons in the fire, to prevent his own infernal kingdom suffering any loss and the heavenly kingdom of Christ having any gain.

He is the same Satan still. There was a godly man who was convinced that his son was drowned. What led him to it I do not know, but he was miles and miles from his home. When he came within sight of his home the first person he saw was his own son. 'Oh!' he said. 'Satan, I've found you a liar. I have again found you a liar. But my loss is that I will believe you again.' For Satan would not come in the same way the next time. Let us not be ignorant of his devices (2 Corinthians 2:11). Especially with regard to hindering the cause of Christ, Satan can make use of these things for the advancement of his own kingdom, and for the weakening of the cause of Christ.

Elisha heard of the matter, and sent word to the king that Naaman be sent to him. No doubt he began to pray about the affair, as a prophet devoted to his God and a patriot devoted to his country. Hearing of the king's distraught condition and the possibility of an impending invasion with more captives taken, he would be spreading the matter before the Lord.

So Naaman came with his retinue and stood at the door of Elisha. Being a leper, he would not want to go in. That is why I think it likely that he had not gone into the palace either, and the letter had been handed in. But now the prophet sent a messenger to him with instructions to go and wash in the River Jordan seven times, and then he would be cured of his leprosy. And now Naaman is angry. First of all the king was in a rage and now it is Naaman's turn. We can see Satan working in order to get Naaman to return. Naaman had his own preconceived ideas as to how he would be healed. He had expected a personal appearance by the prophet and some kind of ceremony. The simplicity of the proposed cleansing was deeply offensive to him. 'So he turned and went away in a rage.' Because things did not turn out as he had expected, he saw no point in obeying the prophet's instructions.

The intemperate anger of the king of Israel and of the Syrian commander were not bad signs. They demonstrated clearly that Satan was afraid. He exerted himself to the utmost to lead them both to false conclusions, and appeared to have succeeded when Naaman went away in a rage. When the Lord goes to work, Satan will be in a rage. But the Lord will fulfil his purposes in spite of Satan, and in spite of the rage of men. The Lord's counsel shall stand, and as Naaman's soul was to be brought to a saving knowledge of God, he subdued the rage of men.

Naaman's servants reasoned with him and, wisely, he acted upon their advice. He got over his rage at the idea of
his going and dipping himself in Jordan, the last place he
would have washed in. John Calvin once said, 'Whoever
will leave the church of Rome, I'm not leaving it.' But
John Calvin *did* later leave the church of Rome and became one of the greatest theologians to expose the doctrines of Rome. We may say many a thing when enraged
and angry, and afterwards see how foolish we were. 'If
any man offend not in word, the same is a perfect man'
(James 5:2). Even Moses the man of God, who was meek
above all men, spoke unadvisedly with his lips. But although a person might be in a rage and say that on no account will they do a certain thing, when the rage subsides
and they get better counsel, they may do it and that will
be to their advantage.

I read somewhere, that the person who admits, 'I made a
mistake and I'm wrong,' is in effect saying, 'I am wiser
today than I was yesterday.' The person who will maintain his attitude he is right at all costs is a person who is
not growing in wisdom. But the person who is ingenuous
and honest enough to admit to being wrong, is in effect
saying, 'I am wiser today than I was yesterday.'

Naaman followed the advice of his attendants, despite his
angry words. He had not really been himself when he was
in a rage. Now when brought to a sober assessment of the
situation, he saw the wisdom of what his servants were
saying. What a blessing that he had such attendants, who
did not say to him, 'Yes, you just carry on and show that
you're not going to dip in their river! What is their Jordan
to our Abana and Pharpar? Just carry on drive at full speed

back to your own land and let them wash in their own river!'

It was a good thing that his attendants were not syco-phants and yes-men. Such advisers are not true friends. What a blessing that Naaman had among his retinue those who sought his advantage, and not persons who were ministering to his pride, and egging him on in the course he was determined to take! Instead they gave him wise counsel to act on the advice of the prophet. And he did.

Naaman dipped seven times in the Jordan and his flesh 'came again like unto the flesh of a little child, and he was clean'. He was completely cured of his leprosy. Then he returned to Elisha's house and wanted to give him some of the presents he had brought, but the prophet would accept nothing. He did not want Naaman to give *him* the glory in any way. The glory of the miracle belonged alone to the Lord.

In the words of our text we have Naaman's confession: 'Behold, now I know that there is no God in all the earth, but in Israel.' We believe that the miracle was blessed to him. The Lord revealed himself to him, and he came to believe in the God of Israel. The Lord can pluck a brand from the burning, just as he saved Saul of Tarsus. He can do a short work in the earth. Naaman had been in the darkness of heathenism, in the darkness of unbelief, but now he says, 'Now I know.'

Christ mentions that there were many lepers in Israel in the days of Elisha the prophet, but none of them was washed save Naaman the Syrian. That shows that the prophet must have had the mind of the Lord in connec-tion with the advice he gave to Naaman to go and wash seven times in Jordan. There was nothing in the waters of Jordan of themselves to cure leprosy. Had these waters been in themselves effective for the curing of leprosy, then Elisha would have told all the lepers in Israel to go and dip in Jordan. But this was the special means appointed by the Lord, through which Naaman was to receive the healing from his leprosy. The Lord uses means—means of his own appointing. These means, which his prophets and teachers set before persons, are to be used. The Lord can bless the means of his own appointment.

In this case the means were for the curing of leprosy, but spiritually the Lord has appointed his own means. We are lepers spiritually. The leprosy of sin has permeated all the faculties of our souls and all the members of our bodies. We have this fatal disease—the leprosy of sin—and we are commanded to make use of the means that the Lord blesses. We are to look to Christ for he has promised to be in his own means, in private and in public, in reading his holy Word and praying to him, and waiting on him, seeking that he would cleanse us. Oh that we would come to him as the leper of old did, who said, 'Lord, if thou wilt, thou canst make me clean!' And Christ said to him. 'I will; be thou clean.'

3. The proofs that Naaman had saving knowledge

In the last place we come to the proofs that Naaman came to a saving knowledge of the God of Israel.

If we have this saving knowledge in our souls, we will know ourselves as lepers—not as good persons. We have the leprosy of sin. And we will confess with the Psalmist: 'For a disease that loathsome is / so fills my loins with pain, / that in my weak and weary flesh / no soundness doth remain' (Psalm 38:7).

We will seek to be washed in Christ's precious blood, and exercise faith in him as the one who can cleanse us from our sins. We will be seeking to pray the prayer of the Psalmist: 'Do thou with hyssop sprinkle me, / I shall be cleansed so; / yea, wash thou me, and then I shall / be whiter than the snow' (Psalm 51:7). Naaman had to go and dip seven times. Seven is the number of perfection. Those who are brought to know themselves as lepers in the presence of the Lord and who are seeking to be cleansed in his precious blood, shall be made perfect in holiness. They shall go on to the very end. It is at death they will be made perfect in holiness. They will need the blood of Christ to be cleansing them from the leprosy of sin till the very end. The leprosy of sin will bring them lower than the grave, to hell, at last, unless they are cleansed from it, and that keeps them waiting at his footstool, seeking to be sanctified and cleansed. That is an evidence of spiritual life in the soul, that a person is seeking to be sanctified—to be cleansed from all filthiness of the flesh and of the spirit, and to perfect holiness in the fear of the Lord.

Naaman requested 'two mules' burden of earth' on which to sacrifice to the Lord. He probably had quite a long interview with the prophet regarding how the God of Israel was to be worshipped. It is mentioned in Ezekiel: 'An altar of earth thou shalt make unto me' (chapter 20:24). Naaman was going to make an altar of earth. He was giving this evidence to the prophet that he was not now going to sacrifice to any other god but to the God of Israel, by taking the earth with him. The sacrifices pointed to

Christ's sacrifice, and his coming put an end to all these sacrifices. Naaman was seeking to worship the Lord as the Lord required at the time. He was giving a bill of divorcement to all the other gods. However religious he had been before now, he saw that his religion had been vain. From now on he was to worship the God of Israel as God required in his Truth.

When you see this desire, it is a mark of spiritual life. Not only is the sinner brought to see himself as a leper—a spiritual leper—needing daily to be washed from the leprosy of sin, but that soul will now seek to worship the Lord in spirit and in truth. He will not say, 'I'll worship the Lord as I see fit myself.' No, he gives the obedience of faith to the God of Israel in the way the Lord himself requires to be worshipped. Any other worship but what is in accordance with his revealed will is simply will-worship. It is unacceptable to him. It is neither to his glory nor to the good of those who indulge in it.

In olden and modern times, when people have gone astray regarding worship, it has proved the thin edge of the wedge, leading to a going astray in doctrine. When the forms of worship become pleasing to the flesh, then people also want doctrines which are pleasing to the flesh. As time passes, they cannot endure sound doctrine, but want what is pleasing to the flesh. We see that in our own day, how corrupt the worship is.

Take, for example, the place given to Christmas. You would almost think that if you didn't keep Christmas, you were not a Christian. Yet there was no word of Christmas in the Christian church till the fourth century. If the keeping of Christmas is the hallmark of a Christian, then the apostles were not Christians and the early martyrs were not Christians, for they never observed Christmas. The very word itself shows it is of popish origin: 'Christ-mass', the mass of Christ. We know that it is just part of the worship of Baal. How often the children of Israel worshipped Baal! They were often seduced by the worship of Baal, and the Church of Rome brought in all these things from Babylon.

The Madonna and her Child that you will see on the 'Christmas' stamps, the sending of cards and presents, the 'Christmas' tree: all this paraphernalia of 'Christmas' is part of the worship of Baal and was brought into the Christian Church by the Church of Rome. In the Reformation Churches, 'Christmas' was done away with, and when the Lord revives his cause, it shall be done away with again.

That is not to say that persons who are truly godly may not become entangled in these vanities. In the third chapter of 2 Corinthians we read of persons who build on Christ the foundation hay, wood and stubble. Instead of building upon the foundation gold and silver and precious stones—that is, what is in accordance with the Lord's Truth—they are building upon the foundation hay, wood and stubble, and it will soon be burnt up. They themselves shall be saved, 'yet so as by fire'. These souls are on the foundation—they are in Christ—but when they engage in work, it is not in accordance with the mind of the Lord. Perhaps *self* is in it: it is all hay, wood and stubble. The conclusions that the king of Israel drew were all hay, wood and stubble. Although he seemed to himself so substantial, his ideas were to a large extent simply his own imaginations. Persons who build on the foundation hay, wood and stubble will have their work burnt up. They will see how foolish they were in their labours—it was labour in vain. All that is not according to God's will shall be burnt up, and only what is precious in *his* sight—the gold and the silver and the precious stones—will stand the fire. 'The fire shall try every man's work of what sort it is.'

We may be supporting something and thinking it is right. The Lord will try it, and if it is not according to his mind he will burn it up. The case of Abraham and Sarah comes to mind. If there was ever a godly person on the foundation laid in Zion, it was Abraham the father of the faithful and his wife Sarah. Yet for a number of years they were trying to hasten the fulfilment of the Lord's promise of a son. On Sarah's advice Abraham took Hagar to wife and a child was born. There was rejoicing at his birth, and they nourished the child and nursed him. They were greatly taken up with this child, and they went on year after year spending their time and labour on this child. The Lord had promised that they would have a son, and now, they thought, this promise was going to be fulfilled. They thought the Lord would accept Ishmael, but all their labour was hay, wood and stubble.

When the Lord's time came, the son of the bondwoman was cast out. He was not to be heir with Isaac. All the years of labour only brought Abraham and Sarah grief and trouble. They had been building hay, wood and stubble on the foundation and thinking all the time that what they were doing was in accordance with the mind of the Lord. How earnestly Abraham besought the Lord for his son! 'O that Ishmael might live before thee!' But all their labour was to be burnt up as if by fire.

With regard to the worship of the Lord, even good men can be building on the foundation with great zeal, yet their work is only hay, wood and stubble that will be burnt up. This is in contrast to the Church in Revelation in her millennial glory—the New Jerusalem. Her foundation is garnished with precious stones. When the millennium comes, all the hay, wood and stubble that even godly people have been putting on the foundation shall be swept aside, and you will find them building upon the foundation nothing but what is in accordance with God's will, and precious in his sight.

It is a good sign when people are led to forsake the hay, wood and stubble of 'Babylon the great'. Although they may have once thought they were doing God service by observing these things, they are brought to see that the Lord will not acknowledge it. It is good to keep to the gold and silver and precious stones in accordance with his Word, as regards worship. 'Great peace have they who love thy law.' There is a blessing in it. But when we become accustomed to contrary ways and give our hearts to them, how grievous it is when they are burnt up! How grievous it was for Abraham when he had to cast out Ishmael! What a wrench to the flesh when we are called to give these things up! But however sore it might be, it is best to submit to the mind of the Lord.

From then on, Naaman was to worship the Lord in accordance with God's Truth. But something came before his mind, and he saw it to be a sin. He was now going back to his own land, and seeing he was the commander-in-chief of the army, it was his duty to accompany the king into the house of Rimmon. Rimmon was the false god of the Syrians. Naaman and the king would have to bow as they entered the temple of Rimmon, and Naaman saw this to be a sin. It was inconsistent with the profession he had just made, that he would only worship the God of Israel from now on. He says twice, 'The LORD pardon thy servant in this thing.'

And Elisha said to him, 'Go in peace.' There is an account in Lachlan Mackenzie's book of a godly Christian woman who said to Mr Mackenzie, 'Is it not strange that the prophet said to Naaman, "Go in peace"?' Mr Mackenzie replied, 'The prophet was right. The prophet knew that grace was but weak in Naaman, and that when grace would grow strong in Naaman, he would relinquish that. Grace would take him out of the temple of Rimmon.'

The prophet left the matter to Naaman himself. This would be a test, as it were. The man seemed to be sincere, so he says, 'Go in peace.' He left the question of the house of Rimmon as Naaman's own responsibility. The prophet would see that Naaman regarded it as a sin, and no doubt he saw that he would not continue in it.

If you turn to 2 Kings 8, you find the prophet Elisha up in Damascus, the capital of Syria. We do not know why Elisha should be there. We may speculate that he went up to see how Naaman was doing, and to see the maid too. However, the maid may have been restored to her home in the land of Israel and her labours rewarded by the Lord, although, to begin with, the mysterious providences that led her to that far country had been incomprehensible. Later on she could see how the Lord was working, and that she had to go there and be the means of bringing Naaman to the knowledge of the Truth.

John Brown of Haddington mentions in his commentary that when Benhadad the king of Syria was sick, he sent Hazael with a present to Elisha, to enquire of the Lord by him whether he should recover. Is it not very strange that it is not Naaman he sent, the man who was a great man with his lord and who had already had contact with the prophet? This would suggest that Naaman had given up his position as commander-in-chief in order that he might worship the God of Israel in spirit and in truth; that he would in no wise countenance idolatry.

That would be another proof of the sincerity of Naaman's confession, that he was determined to follow the Lord through good and through evil report, whatever losses it would entail in connection with prestige or with payment. He would not make an excuse of the requirements of his position. His conscience was made tender, and he would sooner give up his position and the salary which such a position entailed, in order to keep a conscience void of offence toward God and toward men.

May he bless his Truth.

The four lepers

Then they said one to another, We do not well: this day is a day of good tidings, and we hold our peace: if we tarry till the morning light, some mischief will come upon us: now therefore come, that we may go and tell the king's household.

2 KINGS 7:9

I N the preceding chapter we have an account of the siege of Samaria by Benhadad king of Syria and of the great famine that ensued as a result of the siege. In chapter 7 we have an account of the provision which the Lord made to meet the needs of the people of Samaria. 'For the Lord had made the host of the Syrians to hear a noise of chariots, and a noise of horses, even the noise of a great host: and they said one to another, Lo, the king of Israel hath hired against us the kings of the Hittites, and the kings of the Egyptians, to come upon us. Wherefore they arose and fled in the twilight, and left their tents, and their horses, and their asses, even the camp as it was, and fled for their life' (verses 6–7).

ONE THING IS NEEDFUL

It was the Lord's doing. In the first verse of this chapter, Elisha said, 'Hear ye the word of the LORD; Thus saith the LORD, Tomorrow about this time shall a measure of fine flour be sold for a shekel, and two measures of barley for a shekel, in the gate of Samaria.' There would be enough and to spare. We see how scornfully one of the king's lords spoke of Elisha's prophecy.

However, the Syrians fled and left all behind. Four lepers were outside the gates of the city. They could not enter because of their contagious disease. In their extremity they went forward to the camp of the Syrians, hoping that they might get something to keep them alive. To their great surprise, they found all the tents empty and enough there to meet their needs. 'And when these lepers came to the uttermost part of the camp, they went into one tent, and did eat and drink, and carried thence silver, and gold, and raiment, and went and hid it; and came again, and entered into another tent, and carried thence also, and went and hid it.'

After a time it came into their minds that they were not doing well in concealing these good tidings.

In seeking to make a spiritual use of this incident, we may notice in the first place a few things about the day here mentioned. 'This day is a day of good tidings.' It was a day of good tidings in a twofold respect. First, it was a day of good tidings with respect to the provision made to meet the needs of the famishing and perishing inhabitants of Samaria. The provision was of the Lord's doing. It was the Lord who caused the Syrians to hear the noise of horses and chariots, and who caused them to flee and to leave all behind. Apart from this provision the inhabitants of Samaria would have perished from hunger and by the sword of Syria. It was also a day of good tidings in the experience of these four lepers, for they partook of the provision.

Then secondly, we have their confession. They tried to hide what they got, but then it came home to them that this was not right, and they said, 'We do not well.'

In the third place we have their resolution: 'Now therefore come, that we may go and tell the king's household.'

1. A day of good tidings

In the first place, this was 'a day of good tidings'.

An ample provision

It was a day of good tidings with respect to the ample provision that was made. The gospel day is a day of good tidings, in which the provision that the Lord has made in his Son to meet the needs of poor and perishing sinners is set before us.

After the fall man lost all that he had had in a state of innocence. All mankind fell into the spiritual condition reflected by the literal condition of the people of Samaria: shut in to death. That is the condition into which the fall brought mankind. The flaming sword of divine justice which turned every way, shut out man from the blessings which he enjoyed in a state of innocence and closed him in to the death which he incurred by sinning against God. The Lord said, 'In the day that thou eatest thereof thou shalt surely die.' It was when matters were at their darkest that the Lord preached the gospel to Adam and Eve. I heard the late Rev. James Cameron once say that he believed the time between the fall and the giving of the first promise was the darkest period in the history of mankind. There was not a star of hope in the firmament: they were shut in to the eternal death which Adam's sin had procured.

But when the first promise was announced, a star of hope appeared in the firmament. The Lord in the first promise preached the gospel to our first parents. There would come of the seed of the woman the one who would bruise the serpent's head. Christ in all his fulness is the gospel. He is the door of escape and he is the only Saviour. It was Christ who was preached to our first parents in the first promise, and through faith in Christ as set forth in the promise they were delivered from the condemnation that they brought upon themselves.

That was a day of good tidings, when the gospel was first preached in this world, and every time the promise was given after that was a day of good tidings.

It was a day of good tidings when Christ was born into this world. The promises and sacrifices all pointed to his coming in the flesh, and when he was born in Bethlehem the angels sang, 'Behold, we bring you glad tidings of great joy; for this day there is born unto you in the city of David a Saviour who is Christ the Lord.'

It was a day of good tidings when he cried on the cross in connection with the work given him to do, 'It is finished.'

It was a day of good tidings when he rose triumphant over death and the grave.

It was a day of glad tidings when it was said to the women who came to the sepulchre to anoint his body, 'Fear not ye: for I know that ye seek Jesus, which was crucified. He is not here: for he is risen, as he said, Come, see the place where the Lord lay' (Matthew 28:5–6).

It was a day of good tidings when he ascended to the right hand of the Father, as he says to him, 'Sit thou at my right hand, until I make thine enemies thy footstool' (Psalm 110:1).

All that he did in his coming in the flesh—in his obedience unto death, his resurrection and ascension, and glorification—all this is bound up in the glad tidings of the everlasting gospel. So too was the outpouring of the Holy Spirit on the day of Pentecost—the proof that the Holy Spirit was to be in the church till the end of time, making the gospel effectual to the eternal salvation of sinners. That was a day of glad tidings.

It is a day of good tidings for us, as sinners, when we are under the gospel and when we are freely invited to the provision that is spread before us on the table of the gospel. 'All things are now ready; come ye to the feast.' No such glad tidings is to be heard in a lost eternity. There are many who heard the invitation to the feast, and made light of it, who are now in the depths of eternal despair. They would give all that they ever had for another offer of Christ in the gospel. It is a solemn thing to be coming to the means of grace to have Christ offered to us, and to be going away from the means of grace—Sabbath after Sabbath, week after week, year after year—rejecting Christ in the offer of the gospel. It shall yet be laid to the charge of all who die Christless, that they have sinned the sin of rejecting Christ in the gospel offer.

We are invited to come, and told that 'all things are now ready'. How we should be praying to the Lord that he would have mercy upon us, and that he would turn us! 'Turn thou me, and I shall be turned' (Jeremiah 31:18).

An experience of provision

This was a day of good tidings, not only with respect to the provision, but also in the experience of these four lepers. It is one thing to hear the joyful sound; it is another thing to know it. 'O greatly bless'd the people are / the joyful sound that know; / in brightness of thy face, O Lord, / they ever on shall go' (Psalm 89:15).

It is one thing to hear about the provision; it is another thing to be made partakers of it to the saving of our souls. We should not rest content with having the gospel as an outward ordinance. The people of Capernaum had great outward privileges. They heard the gospel from the lips of the Saviour, and they saw the miracles which he performed, which proved that he was the promised Messiah. But although they heard the gospel and saw the miracles, it effected nothing. They went on proudly in their own way. Christ therefore said to them, 'And thou, Capernaum, which art exalted unto heaven' by virtue of the privileges they had above others, 'shalt be brought down to hell' because they repented not (Matthew 11:23).

We may take the four lepers who made the confession and resolution of our text as typifying the Lord's people, who have tasted and been made partakers of the blessings of the everlasting gospel.

Provision for spiritual lepers

First of all we shall observe that it is true of all by nature that we are lepers spiritually. 'From the sole of the foot even unto the head there is no soundness in it; but wounds, and bruises, and putrefying sores' (Isaiah 1:6). The leprosy of sin has permeated all the faculties of our souls and all the members of our bodies. We are altogether as an unclean thing. We are not only lepers, but we are in this perishing condition, just as the people of Samaria were.

We are told what they fed on during the famine in Samaria. 'An ass's head was sold for fourscore pieces of silver, and the fourth part of a cab of dove's dung for five pieces of silver' (2 Kings 6:25). This shows the extremity to which they were reduced, that they were eating that which was unclean. Sheer necessity caused the people of Samaria to eat of that which was unclean. They had nothing else to eat. We see the price they were prepared to pay for this unclean food, to allay the pangs of hunger.

But in the case of man, it is not necessity which causes us, vile sinners that we are, to eat that which is forbidden and unclean. We prove that we have a vicious, depraved appetite on account of sin. The Truth declares that we have a nature that drinks in iniquity like water. We wallow in the mire of sin, just as the sow that has been washed will wallow in the mire again. That is our nature. You can wash the sow as clean as you can, but you have not changed her nature. She will show that her nature has remained unchanged. The first opportunity that presents itself, the sow will go and wallow in the mire again.

That is true of sinners. Whatever outward reformations sinners may make, their nature remains the same. If we cannot wallow actually in the sins on which our heart is set, we will wallow in the mire of sin in our imagination, and drink in iniquity like water. That is proof that we have the leprosy of sin. Sin has destroyed us, and we have no appetite or relish for the things of God.

But the people of Samaria were prepared to give for what was unclean. And what money sinners will spend! What lengths they will go to in spending their money for that which is not bread, and their labour for that which satisfies not! As long as they can get what will gratify their carnal appetites, to what lengths they will go! The Lord in his Truth—in the everlasting gospel—says, 'Wherefore do ye spend money for that which is not bread? and your labour for that which satisfieth not? hearken diligently unto me, and eat ye that which is good, and let your soul delight itself in fatness. Incline your ear, and come unto me: hear, and your soul shall live; and I will make an everlasting covenant with you, even the sure mercies of David' (Isaiah 55:2–3).

By making choice of the pleasures of sin which are but for a season, sinners clearly show what they are. It is not Moses' choice they make. 'This is the condemnation, that light is come into the world, and men loved darkness rather than light, because their deeds were evil' (John 3:19). But when you find those who have made the choice that Moses made, who by faith chose rather to suffer affliction with the people of God than to enjoy the pleasures of sin for a season, you have there persons who have been made partakers of the redemption purchased by Christ—people who have tasted and seen that the Lord is good and gracious, and that Christ and his gospel can meet the needs of their souls.

These four men had discovered they were lepers. Once someone was pronounced to be a leper by the priest they had to be segregated from their homes and from the city. They had to go outside the gate of the city, and if any person came near them, they had to cry out, 'Unclean, unclean!' Others dared not go near them for fear of contracting this dread disease.

It is true, spiritually, that when the Lord convinces a sinner that he is a leper in his sight, that person will go outside the city gate. They go outside the gate of the pleasures of this world, and of the company and association that the person at one time lived in. They are separated. However circumspect we might have been outwardly, the leprosy is within. We should be enquiring whether a sense of our sinnership before God—of our defilement—has caused us to go alone, to be separate, and to be crying out before the Lord for cleansing, 'Unclean, unclean!' Are we crying for forgiveness?

That is true of those who are brought to taste and to see that the Lord is good and gracious, that they are brought to know—some in greater measure than others, as the Lord in his sovereignty sees fit—and to see that they have a disease that is loathsome, and one that will eventually end in eternal death. Their consciousness of it separates them. They *must* go apart. They *must* go outside the gate. No longer are they swallowed up in the life of the city and in the carnal pursuit of the worldly interests that at one time took up their time and energies. They now see the vanity of all these things and the need they have of being prepared for death and eternity.

The lepers came to this extremity. If they entered the city they would perish in the famine. There was nothing in the city for them. They could not go back. There was nothing in the city that would meet their need. There was nothing in the city but death. The people of the city would not receive them; they were outcasts because of their leprosy. On the other hand, if they sat still, they would die also. Hence their resolution: 'Now therefore come, and let us fall unto the host of the Syrians: if they save us alive, we shall live; and if they kill us, we shall but die.'

That was their only hope: to go out to the camp of the Syrians, not knowing whether they would meet pity or death. And so they went forward, knowing that the Syrians would be just in cutting them down—they were lepers and could infect the camp with their leprosy. Or the Syrians might take them for spies sent out from Samaria and put them to death. The four lepers were conscious of all that.

But in going forward they got what they never expected. When these lepers came to the uttermost part of the camp, 'they went into one tent, and did eat and drink, and carried thence silver, and gold, and raiment, and went and hid it'. They found what would meet their need in this provision, and it was the Lord who made this provision.

That is true spiritually. The sinner is brought to see that the Lord would be just in his condemnation—just in cutting him off eternally. His sins deserve eternal death. But when the sinner is brought to justify God, he takes the place that belongs to himself as a poor leper at the foot-stool of the Saviour. That was true literally of the leper when he said to the Saviour, 'Lord, if thou wilt, thou canst make me clean.' And the Lord answered, 'I will; be thou clean.'

Provision in the gospel

It is in Christ, in the provision of the gospel, that the spiritual leper finds cleansing. That is where those, who find themselves to be lepers spiritually, find what will meet their needs as lepers. They find in the Word of God what they found nowhere else. 'Thy words were found, and I did eat them; and thy word was unto me the joy and rejoicing of mine heart: for I am called by thy name, O LORD God of hosts' (Jeremiah 15:16). 'I at thy word rejoice, as one / of spoil that finds great store' (Psalm 119:162).

They found what would suit their case—what would meet their need and satisfy them. There was food and drink here in abundance. There was clothing here for them, and gold and silver. They were satisfied now. There was enough and to spare in this provision to meet their needs.

It is true of God's people that they have found in the gospel what they found nowhere else, and it is to them the joy and rejoicing of their heart. They have tasted that the Lord is good and gracious, and those who have tasted this, seek to feed upon the provision in the gospel. They have Christ as their righteousness. They seek to follow him in this world through good and evil report. They are conscious that they have been delivered from the guilt of sin, for no person could taste that the Lord is good and enjoy his gracious presence in his soul's experience, apart from this deliverance. Others said, 'O who will shew us any good?' (Psalm 4:6). 'Who will show us that which will satisfy us?' All kinds of answers may be given by the men of the world, but the Psalmist knew what would satisfy him. He confesses: 'Upon my heart, bestow'd by thee, / more gladness I have found / than they, ev'n then, when corn and wine / did most with them abound' (Psalm 4:7).

Temporal prosperity can rejoice the heart of those who have a portion in this world only. But whatever temporal prosperity the Lord's people enjoy (and the Lord can grant them that if he sees it to be for their good), of itself that will not satisfy their souls. If the Lord withdraws his gracious presence and they find themselves in bondage and darkness of soul, no worldly wealth or possessions will give them the comfort of which they stand in need. These things will not meet the need of their souls. They know what will meet the need of their souls: to receive provision from the gospel table, to have the Lord lift upon them the light of his countenance and shine on them with his face. That would give them joy of heart that the world knows not of.

The person who seeks that, and is cast down when he does not have it, and is raised up when he has it, is a person whose sin has been pardoned. No person could have that nearness to the Lord if his guilt was still upon him. 'Your iniquities have separated between you and your God' (Isaiah 59:2). It is when the guilt of sin—the cause of separation—is removed, that a sinner has access to the Lord. Then the Lord draws nigh to the sinner and the sinner is enabled to draw nigh to the Lord. When the

guilt has been removed. 'There is therefore now no condemnation to them which are in Christ Jesus, who walk
not after the flesh, but after the Spirit' (Romans 8:1). But
although there is no condemnation, there is still the leprosy of sin in our nature. That is what the apostle describes
in the seventh chapter of Romans, where he speaks of
'another law in my members, warring against the law of
my mind, and bringing me into captivity to the law of sin
which is in my members' (verse 23). It made him cry out,
'O wretched man that I am: who shall deliver me from
the body of this death?' (verse 24).

In this Paul describes the experience of the church of
God, those who have been justified. Although they find
themselves wretched on account of indwelling sin and
corruption, he brings this before them for their comfort:
'There is therefore now no condemnation.' Although
they groan, as the apostle did, on account of their consciousness of indwelling sin, that does not alter the fact
that they are justified persons. Once justified, justified for
all eternity. It is true of those who have tasted that the
Lord is good and gracious that they will be conscious of
the leprosy that is within: 'For a disease that loathsome is
/ so fills my loins with pain, / that in my weak and weary
flesh / no soundness doth remain' (Psalm 38:7).

How Satan can stir up that corruption! How he can bring
before their minds what will satisfy indwelling corruption,
and keep it before their minds! They may go a long time
tempted in that respect, and particularly at a communion
season Satan may mar the good things they have. The
Lord's people are brought to see that they cannot deliver
themselves from such temptations of Satan, for he can not
only tempt them to sin, but he can tempt them in diverse

ways. The Lord will deliver them from the temptations of Satan.

The longer they live in this world, the more they need the prayer, 'Lead us not into temptation.' This petition is towards the end of the Lord's prayer. I believe that to begin with they are taken up with 'Thy kingdom come'. It is true of his people throughout their wilderness journey that they will be praying for the coming of his kingdom in their own souls and the souls of others. And as they go on, they will be praying, 'Give us this day our daily bread'—the bread of life which cometh down from heaven. But as they go on in their wilderness journey, they will see more and more their need of the petition, 'Lead us not into temptation, but deliver us from evil.'

Satan can be at their right hand—and he awaits his opportunity to point out this sin and that other sin of which they have been guilty. Or if they have trespassed, he brings their sins before them and uses them to tempt them. But the Lord will intervene on behalf of his people. He has his own way of intervening and rebuking Satan.

In my own experience, I have discovered that I might receive a wound from an unexpected quarter: a friend, perhaps, who had no idea that he was wounding or hurting me. I could see that the wound would bring me down in myself, and I would say, 'Well, that's the way the Lord took to deliver me from temptation.' We are not to despise the chastening of the Lord, nor faint when we are rebuked of him. We should see the hand of the Lord in whatever we meet with, and say of every bruise or blow or rebuke that may wound us or cast us down, 'Well, the Lord saw that I needed that.'

Nothing comes by chance to the Lord's people. At times the old man may be stirred up in connection with temptation and chastening—that is our nature. But when grace gets into exercise, grace will seek to 'kiss the rod, and him who has appointed it'. The Lord has his own ways of delivering his people from temptation and closing them in to himself. They will be lepers in that respect, that they will need the blood to cleanse them from all sin. They will avail themselves of the prayer of David: 'Do thou with hyssop sprinkle me, / I shall be cleansed so; / yea, wash thou me, and then I shall / be whiter than the snow' (Psalm 51:7).

Abundant provision

What were these tents that the lepers entered, where they found what would satisfy them? There is the tent of the great and precious promises of the Truth, and the tents of the means of grace. They get from the table of the gospel what meets their needs. As the Psalmist said, 'The tabernacles of thy grace / how pleasant, Lord, they be!' (Psalm 84:1). The fellowship of his people is another tent in which they will find what will refresh their souls. The means of grace, the fellowship of his people, and meditation are tents which they seek to enter.

All of this is provided in the everlasting covenant. The further the lepers went into the camp, the more they got. The Lord opens up to his people what is in the covenant. Christ in the everlasting covenant is made unto them of God their wisdom, their righteousness, their sanctification, their redemption.

2. The lepers' confession

In the second place, we shall notice the lepers' confession. What they got they hid. They thought they were acting very wisely in hiding what they got. But it was not to hide it that they were given this provision. It was the Lord who made the provision, and it was the Lord who led them to get what would meet their needs in these tents. Now, they thought it was their wisdom to hide what they got; they would keep it to themselves. But it was brought home to them that they were not doing right. The condition of their fellow citizens in Samaria came home upon them: they were famishing, while here was enough and to spare. Were they going to hide and keep to themselves what could meet the needs of their fellows?

They came to confess, 'We do not well.' They had thought they were doing well, and acting wisely and prudently, but now they are brought to say, 'We do not well; this day is a day of good tidings, and we hold our peace: if we tarry till the morning light, some mischief will come upon us.' 'Some mischief', which means 'some punishment'. They found that they would be guilty if they continued hiding what they got. They got what they got in the tents of the Syrians in order that they might make it known to others.

3. The lepers' resolution

Then we have their resolution. 'Come, that we may go and tell the king's household.' Whether the king's household would accept their report or not, they felt that they were doing their duty in telling them what they got. We see them going to tell the king's household—those in authority—who ordered that investigation should be made regarding what they were saying. At first the king came to the conclusion that it was just a plot—part of the Syrians' strategy, so that when the people of Samaria would open the gates the Syrians would return unexpectedly and capture them. So, it was decided that investigation should be made. 'Let us send and see.' This investigation cast no reflection on the lepers. The king's officers were duty bound to see to the safety of the city, and it might well be that there was a plot.

This is also true spiritually, in connection with people making known what the Lord has done for their souls. They cannot deny that they found in the Word of God what revived and refreshed their souls. They were enabled to say with the Psalmist, 'All that fear God, come, hear, I'll tell / what he did for my soul' (Psalm 66:16). They have a hope that the Lord did meet with them and deliver them. It is a duty, nevertheless, for the minister and elders to investigate their profession for the honour and good of the cause.

I mentioned previously the case of John Morrison, who was a noted believer in Harris in the last century. He was well known in his day and generation, a great Gaelic poet. He came to a communion season on the Isle of Skye in the days of the eminent minister, Rev. Roderick Macleod. John Morrison, who was known as 'the Harris Bard', did not make himself known. He waited behind after the service on the Saturday for a token. He was told to wait, seeing he was a stranger, to be examined by the Kirk Session. Of course, John Morrison could answer all the questions put. He was told that they were fully satisfied with his knowledge and his experience. 'But,' they said, 'seeing you are a stranger to us and we do not know how you are living, we deem it prudent not to give you the token. For we do not know how you may be living, although you are so well acquainted with the Scriptures, and could answer all things as to experience.'

John Morrison turned round and lifted his hands and said, 'Glory be to thee, O Lord, that there is a person in Scotland that has such a regard for the honour of thine house!' When the Session heard what he said, they called him back and gave him a token, and it was then he made known to them who he was.

Those who are the king's officers, spiritually, have their duty to the Lord's cause, to seek to uphold the cause. They have to do so faithfully and in the spirit of meekness. These two qualities are joined in the Truth: righteousness and meekness. 'Seek righteousness, seek meekness' (Zephaniah 2:3). This command is given because we are so prone to separate what God has joined. If we are righteous and faithful, and yet do not evince a spirit of meekness, we have discharged our duty in a way that satisfies ourselves, and we think it will satisfy the Lord too. But if we separate what the Lord has joined, then however faithful or righteous we may appear to be, it cannot be well-pleasing to the Lord, seeing we have separated what the Lord has joined. We are to seek righteousness and seek meekness. Christ himself says that he is 'meek and lowly in heart'.

We find the apostle Paul—and who more faithful than he?—seeking to uphold the honour and the good of the cause of Christ in Corinth. He had to rebuke them for how matters were in the church there, in connection with the administration of the sacrament, discipline and other matters. This is how he addresses them: 'Now I Paul myself beseech you by the meekness and gentleness of Christ, who in presence am base among you.' 'You may think little of me,' he says—and they did think little of him, for they did not think he was an apostle, because he had not seen the Lord in the flesh as the other apostles had. But he discharges his duty with all fidelity and righteousness in connection with the honour of Christ's cause in Corinth. And as he did so, it was on this he was laying emphasis: the meekness and gentleness of Christ (2 Corinthians 10:1).

It is our nature to assert ourselves, but a meek spirit is in the sight of God of great price. By asserting ourselves we foolishly think that we must be being faithful, but a meek and quiet spirit is in the sight of God of great price.

Meekness is a fruit of spirituality. The Lord not only joins it to righteousness, but also with spirituality: 'Brethren, if a man be overtaken in a fault, ye which are spiritual, restore such an one in the spirit of meekness; considering thyself, lest thou also be tempted' (Galatians 6:1). The more spiritually-minded a person is, the more he will have of the Spirit of Christ, who is 'meek and lowly in heart', and the more he will have of the spirit of the apostle when, discharging faithfully his duty in connection with the cause of Christ in Corinth, he besought them by the meekness and gentleness of Christ. Paul was not lording it over them, or vaunting his authority as an apostle. He was willing to be base in their estimation as long as everything would be done in a way that would be to the glory of the Lord and for the good of his cause.

The king's officers have to deal with matters pertaining to his cause in the right manner. As well as righteousness and faithfulness there must be the spirit of meekness, which is in the sight of God of great price. Meekness is an evidence of spirituality, for when the carnal mind gets the upper hand, even in a gracious person—and that is what Satan seeks—then the spirit of meekness retires. It is one's own spirit that is then uppermost, and when one's own spirit is uppermost, then we may think that not acting in accordance with meekness is nonetheless acting faithfully. Then we are guilty of separating what the Lord has joined. 'Seek righteousness, seek meekness.'

The apostle says to Timothy, 'The servant of the Lord must not strive (that is, be contentious); but be gentle unto all men, apt to teach, patient, in meekness instructing those that oppose themselves' (2 Timothy 2:24–25). There was hope for even those who opposed themselves, that they might be recovered from the snare of the devil, for the Lord will bless the means he is prescribing. The instruction given, even to those who oppose themselves, must be in patience and in meekness: in other words, speaking the truth in love.

We see how the king's officers investigated the case, in faithfulness to the city and the good of the inhabitants. That is also to be true spiritually, and illustrates the spirit which is to characterise the King's household in connection with them discharging their duty toward his cause in this world. This is well-pleasing in his sight and precious in his sight.

The Lord had need of these lepers for the fulfilment of this promise: 'Tomorrow about this time shall a measure of fine flour be sold for a shekel, and two measures of barley for a shekel, in the gate of Samaria.' Humanly speaking, and speaking with all reverence, that promise would have fallen to the ground were it not for these four lepers. The Lord had need of them to make known this provision and thus, in the ruling of his providence, to have this prophecy fulfilled.

The Lord's Supper is a sign and seal of blessings to come for the Lord's people. When instituting the Supper, the Saviour said that his people were to do this in remembrance of him, 'till he come'. The Lord's Supper has been commemorated since it was instituted in the upper room in Jerusalem until this time, and it shall continue to be observed in the church of God until the end of the world. It points us forward to what the Word of God prophesies, the second coming of Christ.

Now, again speaking with reverence, that prophecy would fall to the ground were it not for the Lord's people following the path of duty, in telling the King's household and publicly making known what the Lord has done for their souls. The Lord has need of his people, as he had need of the four lepers, to make known the provision and also for the fulfilment of his prophecy. He makes use of his people for the fulfilling of that prophecy, as they commemorate his death until he come.

May he bless his Truth.

The blessedness of God's people

Blessed is the man whom thou choosest, and causest to approach unto thee, that he may dwell in thy courts: we shall be satisfied with the goodness of thy house, even of thy holy temple.

PSALM 65:4

WE shall notice in the first place that God has opened up a way whereby sinners can approach unto him. In the second place, we shall notice a few things implied in the Lord causing a sinner to approach unto him. In the third place we shall notice the blessedness of the person whom the Lord causes to approach unto him. In the fourth and last place, a mark or two—proofs and evidences—of those who are thus blessed, whom the Lord has chosen and caused to approach unto himself.

1. The way God has opened for sinners

First of all, the words of our text bring before us the fact that God has opened up a way whereby sinners can approach unto him. In a state of innocence man could approach unto God by way of a covenant of works, on the ground of that obedience which God required of him according to the tenor of the covenant. Man being created holy in the image of God, he was able to give that perfect and sinless obedience to God's law which God required of him. He was giving obedience to the command, 'Do this, and thou shalt live.' While he continued to give the obedience God required of him, he enjoyed communion and fellowship with God.

But we see how man fell from the estate in which he was created, by sinning against God. Through the fall of man the way of approach to God was closed. Man lost the image of God, he lost the holiness and the righteousness and the knowledge which he had in a state of innocence, and he came under the power of spiritual death. As the Lord had said, 'In the day that thou eatest thereof thou shalt surely die.'

And Adam died spiritually that day. He lost the spiritual life that he had. He lost God as his portion. He lost the image of God. He became liable to temporal death, and to eternal death in hell. He proved that he had no desire now to approach God. His desire now was to flee from God. Instead of being spiritually minded, as he had been in a state of innocence, when he had found it good to be drawing nigh unto God and enjoying his fellowship and communion, Adam now became carnally minded.

The Truth says that 'to be carnally minded is death' (Romans 8:6). Adam now came under the power of sin, under the power of spiritual death, and under the power of Satan. That was true not only of Adam on the day in which he sinned, it is true of every individual of Adam's lost race—it is true of you and of me as we are by nature.

We are carnally minded. That expression aptly describes the spiritual condition of every sinner until he is reconciled to God and made a new creature in Christ Jesus. 'The carnal mind is enmity against God; for it is not subject to the law of God, neither indeed can be' (Romans 8:7).

To be carnally minded is to be fleshly minded. The person is under the dominion of the lusts of the flesh, the lust of the eye, and the pride of life. These are the sinful principles that operate in the minds of sinners as they are by nature—not holy principles, but carnal and sinful principles. The dominion of such principles in the soul of a sinner shows that he is without God and without hope in the world. He is in a state of enmity against God. In this condition it is impossible to please God. 'So then they that are in the flesh cannot please God' (Romans 8:8). 'Who can bring a clean thing out of an unclean? Not one.' They may please themselves and think they are pleasing God by doing this, that and the other, but all who are in the flesh *cannot* please God. Nothing will please God but the finished work of the Lord Jesus Christ—the righteousness which he wrought out. Your soul and my soul must be clothed upon with the righteousness of Christ, we must be made new creatures in Christ Jesus, if we are to be well-pleasing in God's sight. It is only in Christ that sinners are accepted. They are said to be 'accepted in the beloved' (Ephesians 1:6).

Having proved that he was carnally minded and had lost the spirituality of mind and of soul that he had had, man was now fleeing from God instead of seeking to draw nigh to God—seeking to hide himself from God, and trying to banish the thought of God out of his mind.

101

Multitudes of sinners try to hide from themselves the idea of God. It disturbs them. The idea of the God of justice which the Truth brings before us disturbs them, and they have recourse to a denial of God. They try to hide themselves, as Adam tried to hide himself behind the trees of the garden. They try to hide themselves behind the tree of atheism, or the tree of infidelity, and they try to make out that there is no God. The Word of God tells of such, 'The fool hath said in his heart, There is no God' (Psalm 14:1).

There was a godly old man called Angus Graham, a Free Presbyterian. A man came to him and wanted something to read. The old man gave him a good book or a good magazine. 'Read that,' he said. The other glanced at it. 'Oh,' he said. 'I've no place for religion. I don't believe there is a God. I don't want any of that stuff.' Mr Graham looked at him and said, 'Do you know what God in his Word says about you?' 'No,' replied the infidel. 'He says you're a fool.' It is proof of the carnal mind being enmity against God that if man could, he would simply banish God out of existence.

There are multitudes more who seek to hide themselves behind a false image of God. They have a God of their own imagination, not the God of truth. They worship this God of their own imagination—a God that is all mercy and all love. This is the sop they give to their consciences and they think that God is like themselves. As the Lord says, 'These things hast thou done, and I kept silence; thou thoughtest that I was altogether such an one as thyself' (Psalm 50:21). That is the kind of God that multitudes worship; a God that will approve of their sins, not the God of truth who condemns sinners to the lowest hell. They want to banish the true God out of their minds. They think that they can hide behind an image— the image of a false god that will approve of their sins and allow them to live as they list. The Lord speaks solemnly to such. 'Consider this, ye that forget God, lest I tear you in pieces, and there be none to deliver' (Psalm 50:22).

We are called upon to abandon all such views. We are just fooling ourselves and deceiving ourselves for eternity, trying to hide behind the image of some false god, a god of our own imagination.

So sinners prove in one way or another that they have no desire to draw nigh unto God, to approach unto him. The desire of their hearts is, 'Depart out of our coasts. We desire not the knowledge of thy ways. We desire the knowledge of our own ways. It is our own ways that we will choose, it matters not how contrary these are to God's ways.' Sinners show thereby that they have no true desire to approach God.

That is the condition in which man is spiritually as he is by nature: spiritually dead, with no desire to approach unto God.

We see also that after man fell, the flaming sword which turned every way was placed to guard the way to the tree of life. The flaming sword of God's justice was shutting sinners out. Man closed the way by his sin; God closed the way in judgment and in justice. The flaming sword was there as proof that man was shut out from the way of life.

And man would have been shut out for all eternity, had not God in his love and mercy opened up a new and a living way whereby sinners could approach him. It is of God that such a way has been opened. After the fall, Adam and Eve heard the voice of the Lord God walking in the garden in the cool of the day. It is a person they heard walking, called 'the Voice of the Lord' or 'the Word of the Lord'. 'The Word' is one of the glorious titles of the Lord Jesus Christ. As we read, 'In the beginning was the Word, and the Word was with God, and the Word was God' (John 1:1). 'And the Word was made flesh, and dwelt among us, (and we beheld his glory, the glory as of the only begotten of the Father,) full of grace and truth' (John 1:14).

It was Christ who came forth, God in the person of the Son, to make known to Adam this new and living way. The new way of access—of approach unto God—was opened to Adam in the first promise. God said in the first place to Satan by way of condemnation, and in the way of a promise to Adam, 'There shall come of the seed of the woman who shall bruise the serpent's head.' The seed of the woman has reference to the incarnation of Christ, to his virgin birth. He was to be of the seed of the woman, not of the seed of the man. He was conceived miraculously by the power of the Holy Ghost in the womb of the virgin Mary, and born of her, yet without sin. 'Behold, a virgin shall conceive, and bear a son, and shall call his name Immanuel' (Isaiah 7:14).

The Son of God was manifested that he might destroy the works of the devil. By his atoning death he destroyed 'him that had the power of death, that is, the devil' (Hebrews 2:14). It is sin which gave the devil power over mankind, and it is through sin being atoned for, that Satan could lose his power. Man was given over to the devil in judgment—that was part of the punishment man incurred through sinning against God. He sold himself to sin and to Satan. Regarding sin God said, 'The soul that sinneth it shall die.' 'In the day that thou eatest thereof thou shalt surely die.' God is not a man, that he should lie (Numbers 23:19). What the God of truth has said shall stand.

God in his love and mercy found out the way whereby sin could be condemned unto death—the sentence of death could be executed and yet the sinner set free. He sent his only begotten Son to endure that death, the death due to the sins of all that shall be saved. Christ died for our sins according to the Scriptures; by his death he spoiled principalities and powers, and made a show of them openly through his cross.

That was opened up to Adam in the first promise and in the sacrifice that the Lord God offered. Adam and Eve were clothed with the skins of animals slain in sacrifice. Thus the scheme of redemption was opened up and Christ was set forth typically in the sacrifice offered immediately after the fall. Christ was likewise set forth in the other sacrifices of the Old Testament church. It was when Christ came in the flesh, and finished the work given him to do—when he cried on the cross, 'It is finished'—it was then that the way was actually opened up. We read that when he cried these words, 'It is finished,' the veil of the temple was rent from top to bottom, indicating that the new and living way was now opened up.

Christ himself, in all his fulness, is the way of approach to God. As he declares, 'I am the way, the truth, and the life: no man cometh unto the Father, but by me' (John 14:6). He is the only way. Therefore we are called upon to seek

ONE THING IS NEEDFUL

Christ. As we are by nature, we are out of the way, but he is able to enlighten us and bring us into the way. He 'can have compassion on the ignorant, and on them that are out of the way' (Hebrews 5:2). We should be praying that the Lord would open our eyes to see that we are out of the way, and that he would lead us into the only way— that we would find Christ.

2. The Lord makes sinners approach him

We shall notice in the second place a few things implied in the Lord causing a sinner to approach him. It is because Christ by his obedience opened up this new and living way that sinners can approach God. 'Blessed is the man whom thou choosest, and causest to approach unto thee.' The Lord causes him to approach unto himself.

The sinner, as we have already mentioned, has no desire to approach unto God. The sinner is in the far country, far off from God. 'Your sins have separated between you and your God.' He is either engrossed in riotous living, like the prodigal son, or absorbed in the affairs of this world, unconcerned whether he is in the narrow way that leads to life, and quite forgetful of the solemn fact that he is on the broad way that leads to everlasting destruction. He has a god of his own imagination and he pays homage of a kind to this god—a god that will allow him to carry on as he likes himself. He gives a sop to his conscience by giving a worship of some kind to his god. His stance is, 'God is merciful, and all shall be well in the end.' Well, God *is* merciful. 'The Lord our God is merciful, / and he is gracious, / long-suffering, and slow to wrath, / in mercy plenteous' (Psalm 103:8). But God is only gracious in Christ; God is only merciful in Christ. You will not taste a drop of mercy in time or in eternity apart from being found in Christ. You are building upon a foundation of sand if you are building upon the general mercy of God, for he is only reconciled in Christ.

It is of the Lord that any sinner is caused to approach unto him. If man was left to his own free will, he would just go on to the end. But we have here before us in the Word, 'Blessed is the man whom thou *causest* to approach unto thee.' It is of the Lord that any sinner in truth approaches to the Most High. The Lord causes the sinner to approach.

There is implied in these words the efficacious and the gracious teaching of the Holy Spirit. Apart from the Holy Spirit we shall remain ignorant of Christ and of ourselves, and of all that pertains to our everlasting salvation. 'The natural man receiveth not the things of the Spirit of God: for they are foolishness unto him: neither can he know them, because they are spiritually discerned' (1 Corinthians 2:14).

We need spiritual discernment, divine and supernatural teaching, to know the things pertaining to our everlasting peace. The sinner is duty bound to approach the Lord. The Lord calls upon sinners to draw nigh unto him and to turn from their evil ways to the Lord. Sinners who ignore these invitations and warnings thereby only add to their own condemnation. It is a solemn thing to hear the gospel and to have the Word of God in our hands. In virtue of such privileges we are raised to the very gates of heaven, as the people of Capernaum were, to whom Christ said that they would be cast down into hell because they did not repent.

'No man', says Christ, 'can come unto me, except the Father which hath sent me draw him' (John 6:44). In the Lord causing a sinner to approach unto him, there is the drawing of the Father through the teaching of the Holy Spirit. 'Ye will not come to me,' said the Saviour, 'that ye might have life.' Sinners have no will—no mind—to come. 'This is the condemnation, that light is come into the world, and men loved darkness rather than light, because their deeds were evil' (John 3:19). That is what sinners choose by nature—the ways of darkness and of sin, in preference to the light. Man's inability to come to God is proof of the condemnation of his state, proof that he is under the power of spiritual death, under the power of sin and of Satan.

People may make an excuse of their inability. 'What can I do? I am unable to do anything spiritually good.' But if that is your excuse, it is the clearest proof that you are a condemned sinner, for all who are taught by the Holy Spirit are brought to mourn over their inability. Their inability is their unbelief. We read that when the Holy Spirit comes, he convinces 'of sin, because they believe not on me'. You are altogether sinful, your mind is altogether averse to the things of the Spirit of God.

When the Lord deals with the sinner, he is brought to himself. We read of the prodigal son in the far country, that he came to himself. And when he did, he said, 'I will arise and go to my father's house.' It is of the Lord that any sinner is brought to that. The sinner whom he causes to approach unto him, sees that he is a sinner. He is now convinced that he is a sinner and that the God of the Bible is the God of truth, that he himself is accountable to the God of truth, that he is condemned because of his sin, and that God will be just in his eternal condemnation.

One time when the great George Whitefield was preaching, after the sermon a lady said, 'Does he think that the Lord would send such a respectable person as I am to hell?' All the godliness that some people have is their respectability. But however respectable a person may be—however moral outwardly—until he is found in Christ he is under condemnation. He is condemned already. He is full of sin. He is under the power of the carnal mind which is enmity against God, which is not subject to his law, neither indeed can be.

The sinner whom the Lord causes to approach unto him is brought to see that, and to confess, 'If thou, LORD, shouldest mark iniquities, O Lord, who shall stand?' (Psalm 130:3). He is brought before the Lord as the publican was, beating upon his breast and crying out, 'God be merciful to me a sinner.'

Think of Saul of Tarsus. In his own estimation he was blameless according to the righteousness of the law. Blameless outwardly, he was yet brought to see himself as the chief of sinners. That is true of any whom the Lord causes to approach unto himself: it is as a sinner that he draws nigh. 'This man receiveth sinners, and eateth with them' (Luke 15:2). 'I am not come to call the righteous, but sinners to repentance' (Matthew 9:13).

The prodigal son was a sinner in his own estimation when he set his face towards the father's house and turned his back on the far country. This was also true of the publican in the temple when he was smiting his breast and crying, 'God be merciful to me a sinner.'

The Lord causes the sinner to approach unto him as a righteous judge. The sinner sees God to be just in his condemnation, but he is also brought to see that Christ is the way, the truth and the life. In the Lord causing him to draw nigh, the sinner is being brought to Christ. 'No man can come to me, except the Father which hath sent me draw him: and I will raise him up at the last day' (John 6:44).

The sinner is brought to trust and hope in Christ, and to follow Christ in this world through good and through evil report. This is the fruit of his being elected and chosen. It is not because of any good in a person that he was caused to approach unto the Lord. There is no difference, for all have sinned and come short of the glory of God. When a sinner is brought to a saving knowledge of the Lord Jesus, that flows from God's sovereign pleasure and his will concerning that person before the foundation of the world. That person was elected in Christ before the foundation of the world. As the apostle says, 'Who hath saved us, and called us with an holy calling, not according to our works, but according to his own purpose and grace, which was given us in Christ Jesus before the world began' (2 Timothy 1:9).

Their election comes to light in effectual calling, in being drawn effectually to Christ, in the Lord causing them to approach unto him. He causes them to see themselves as they are—lost and ruined and hell-deserving. And he closes them in to Christ as the way, as the truth and as the life. Christ becomes to them the way. He becomes to them the manifestation of truth. And he is their life. They are chosen out of the world that lieth in the wicked one. As Christ says, 'If ye were of the world, the world would love his own: but because ye are not of the world, but I have chosen you out of the world, therefore the world hateth you' (John 15:19). They are separated from the companions they once had, and from the ways they once pursued, and from the pleasures of sin, which are but for a season. As surely as the prodigal son was separated from the riotous living in the far country, so they are separated from these sinful pleasures.

That is true of every person whom the Lord causes to approach unto him. It flows in the first place from his eternal election. That person was chosen in Christ from the foundation of the world, and not for any good in himself. His election was all according to God's sovereign good pleasure. It comes to light when the Lord draws that person nigh unto himself, and causes him to turn his back on the world. He now makes choice of that good part which shall not be taken from him. As Christ says to his own, 'Ye have not chosen me, but I have chosen you, and ordained you, that ye should go and bring forth fruit.'

3. The blessedness of the person the Lord chooses

In the next place, consider the blessedness of the person 'whom thou choosest, and causest to approach unto thee'.

He is a blessed person. It is true of him that he will have this prayer as long as he is in this world: 'Draw me, and we will run after thee.' He is conscious of the spiritual death in his own soul, for he has the old nature still. He has both the new nature and the old. The flesh wars against the spirit, and the spirit against the flesh. These two are contrary one to the other. The Lord's own people are so conscious of spiritual deadness and their need of

111

being quickened and drawn, that this is their constant prayer and desire: 'Draw me, and we shall run after thee.'

Justification

They are a blessed people. The soul whom the Lord has caused to approach unto him has the blessing of justification. He is justified in God's sight. The drawing to Christ is his effectual calling, and all who are called effectually are justified. 'Whom he called, them he also justified: and whom he justified, them he also glorified' (Romans 8:30). They are justified in God's sight: that is, their sins are forgiven them and they are accepted as righteous. 'Justification is an act of God's free grace, wherein he pardoneth all our sins, and accepteth us as righteous in his sight, only for the righteousness of Christ imputed to us, and received by faith alone' (Shorter Catechism, Q. 33)

If the Lord brought you nigh to him and you tasted in your soul that the Lord is good and gracious, and Christ became precious to you and you are now seeking to follow him, then your desire will be to get nearness of soul to him. You mourn over the death that you find in your soul and the darkness you find in your soul. That is an evidence that you are justified. It is an evidence that the cause of separation between you and God has been removed. Sin is the cause of separation. The guilt of sin is the cause of condemnation. 'There is therefore now no condemnation to them which are in Christ Jesus, who walk not after the flesh, but after the Spirit.' They are justified and they prove it too, not only by their access to the Lord. That is offered as a proof of justification by the apostle. 'Therefore being justified by faith, we have peace with God through our Lord Jesus Christ: by whom also

THE BLESSEDNESS OF GOD'S PEOPLE

we have access by faith into this grace wherein we stand, and rejoice in hope of the glory of God' (Romans 5:1–2).

They now seek to draw nigh, and they find access to God through Christ in their souls' experience. Although they have to complain how far off they find themselves to be, they still have access to God in Christ. He who came to rest and trust in Christ is a justified person. Sin—and the guilt of sin, which came between his soul and God in Christ—has been blotted out, and the righteousness of Christ put to his account. The proof of that is not only that he seeks access to God, but that the language of his soul is, 'O that I might be found in Christ, not having mine own righteousness which is of the law, but the righteousness which is through the faith of Christ; the righteousness which is of God by faith.' He sees that all his own righteousnesses are as filthy rags and that nothing will stand him for eternity but to have Christ as his righteousness.

Adoption

He has also the blessing of adoption. He is now adopted into God's family; he will dwell in the courts of God's house. And he has the spirit of adoption, whereby he is enabled to cry, 'Abba, Father.' He has a love to the family of God. 'We know that we have passed from death unto life, because we love the brethren' (1 John 3:14). The Lord's people have a heart-attachment to the brethren and to the courts of God's house.

Sanctification

They also have the blessing of sanctification. They are being sanctified. This work is a process that is going on, and it is at death that they will be made perfect in holiness and the work of sanctification brought to completion. You can find the work of sanctification in the confession that the blessed man has: 'Iniquities prevail against me; as for our transgressions, thou shalt purge them away.'

This people are concerned about their iniquities and the sinfulness of their nature. Yet they are looking to the Lord as the one who can purge them and cleanse them. They are therefore daily praying with the Psalmist, 'Do thou with hyssop sprinkle me, / I shall be cleansed so; / yea, wash thou me, and then I shall / be whiter than the snow' (Psalm 51:7).

Glorification

This is implied in their blessedness: at death they shall be glorified. They shall go to be forever with the Lord, 'Whom he justified, them he also glorified.'

4. Evidences of those who are blessed

In the last place, a mark or two of those who are declared blessed by the Lord.

One mark is that they dwell in his courts. They have a heart-attachment to God's house. With the Psalmist they confess, 'One thing I of the Lord desir'd, / and will seek to obtain, / that all days of my life I may / within God's house remain' (Psalm 27:4). 'A day in thy courts is better than a thousand. I had rather be a doorkeeper in the house of my God, than to dwell in the tents of wicked-ness' (Psalm 84:10).

'We shall be satisfied with the goodness of thy house, even of thy holy temple.' That is the provision of the gospel. They are satisfied with the everlasting gospel of our

Lord and Saviour Jesus Christ. When Christ was preaching the doctrines of the gospel, the multitude said, 'This is an hard saying; who can hear it?' They wanted to make him king, and you would think they had great zeal in following Christ, but when he began to preach to them the doctrines of the gospel, they went back and walked no more with him. They did not want to be satisfied with the goodness of his house. They were quite content as long as he would feed them with loaves and fishes, and perform miracles for their bodily comfort. They did not want his doctrines.

We are told clearly that the time would come when people would not endure sound doctrine. They will not put up with it; they will want other doctrine. They will heap up to themselves other teachers who will give them unsound doctrine, and tell them that God is a God of love and mercy and that all shall be well in the end. They will have abundance of these teachers, because they cannot endure sound doctrine. But a person who cannot endure sound doctrine is still on the way to hell. He is on the broad road. He is blind. He is not of the blessed people mentioned in our text, who are satisfied with the goodness of the Lord's house.

Christ says in the everlasting gospel, 'Wherefore do ye spend money for that which is not bread? and your labour for that which satisfieth not? Hearken diligently unto me, and eat ye that which is good, and let your soul delight itself in fatness' (Isaiah 55:2). 'That which is good' is the gospel, and Christ himself in the gospel. When you look around today, you see how poor sinners are spending their money seeking satisfaction, and they never get it. They'll try this, and they'll try that, and they're hoping to get what will satisfy them, but they will not. 'Incline your ear,' Christ says, 'and come unto me: hear, and your soul shall live; and I will make an everlasting covenant with you, even the sure mercies of David' (Isaiah 55:3). The person that is blessed is satisfied with the gospel. He does not want any other gospel but the everlasting gospel of our Lord and Saviour Jesus Christ. He knows that if there is anything for his soul, it is on the table of the gospel. Sometimes he gets a crumb of the bread of life from the table of the gospel; other times he feels himself destitute. Yet even then he knows that there is enough and to spare for him on the table of the gospel. It is at 'times convenient' that the Lord bestows on them their food.

There is also this mark of the blessed people, that they seek to praise the Lord. This is their confession: 'Praise waiteth for thee, O God, in Zion: and unto thee shall the vow be performed' (Psalm 65:1). They are a praising people. They live to praise him in Sion's daughter's gates. They will want a new song in their mouths to be praising the Lord for his works and his wonders done unto them and to the sons of men. Part of praise is to be paying our vows unto the Lord. As we read, 'Offer unto God thanksgiving; and pay thy vows unto the most High' (Psalm 50:14). Their paying their vows is a rendering of thanksgiving unto the Lord. As the Psalmist says, 'What shall I render to the Lord / for all his gifts to me?' He then goes on to say, 'I'll of salvation take the cup, / on God's name will I call: / I'll pay my vows now to the Lord / before his people all' (Psalm 116:14)

The last mark that I shall mention regarding the blessed person is his exercise of soul in connection with going to pay his vows. He says, 'Thou that hearest prayer, unto

thee shall all flesh come. Iniquities prevail against me: as
for our transgressions, thou shalt purge them away' (Psalm
65:2–3). He feels himself coming so far short in offering
praise and paying his vows; and when confronted with his
solemn duty, he turns to the Lord. 'O thou that hearest
prayer, unto thee shall all flesh come.' The word 'flesh',
according to some, is to be understood as 'man in his
weakness and helplessness'. The person saying this is finding himself as the apostle did when he said, 'O wretched
man that I am! who shall deliver me from the body of this
death?' 'I feel so carnal, sold under sin, so fleshly, and so
far from what I should be.' He is in effect saying, 'To
whom shall I go but unto thee?' He is conscious of his
sinfulness when setting his face on holy and solemn duties.
We have it in the Word here, and in our personal experience. When viewing the holy duty of rendering his vows
unto the Lord, this is what confronts him, This is how he
finds himself and he cries to the hearer of prayer, 'Iniquities, I must confess, / prevail against me do.' He finds
himself so weak and helpless. 'But as for our transgressions, / them purge away shalt thou.' Faith there looks to
the Saviour, the Advocate within the veil, the one who
paid the ransom price, and who is the propitiation for our
sins, and not for ours only, but for the sins of the whole
world. The soul seeks cleansing and purging and preparation for holy duties.

That then is a portrait of the blessed man. You are the
blessed man; you are the person who has reason to go and
pay his vows unto the Lord. That is experimentally in
some measure what the Holy Spirit here says of the person that he describes as blessed. Others may be confessing
how full they are of love and faith. But the blessed person
may well find himself how the apostle found himself on

the threshold of glory, crying, 'O wretched man that I am!'

The more that grace advances in the soul, the more a person becomes conscious of the depravity of his nature. The more light that enters the soul, the more darkness and sin the person sees. That poor person might conclude, 'Oh, it is impossible that I am blessed—such a person as I am!' But you see, this sense of sin is a mark of the person that the Lord is describing as blessed: the soul whom he has caused to approach unto him, whom he has brought into his courts, and who will be satisfied with the goodness and fatness of his house, even of his holy place.

We should be praying to the Lord that he would grant us this blessing, and that we would not be left to ourselves. He says, 'I will be enquired of by the house of Israel, to do these things for them.' He desires that sinners will ask that he would do this for them, for the things that are impossible with men are possible with God.

Set your face therefore upon the throne of grace and cry to the Lord. Because he has opened up a new and living way, and is saying in the Truth, 'This is the way, walk ye in it.' Pray that the Lord would put you in the way. Pray that he would have mercy upon you and teach and enlighten you. This is his delight. This is the work on which he has set his heart: the saving of sinners. 'This is a faithful saying, and worthy of all acceptation, that Christ Jesus came into the world to save sinners; of whom I am chief' (1 Timothy 1:15). And he himself says, 'Him that cometh unto me I will in no wise cast out' (John 6:37).

May he bless his Truth.

Baruch

Thus saith the LORD, the God of Israel, unto thee, O Baruch; Thou didst say, Woe is me now! for the LORD hath added grief to my sorrow; I fainted in my sighing, and I find no rest. Thus shalt thou say unto him, The LORD saith thus; Behold, that which I have built will I break down, and that which I have planted I will pluck up, even this whole land. And seekest thou great things for thyself? seek them not: for, behold, I will bring evil upon all flesh, saith the LORD: but thy life will I give unto thee for a prey in all places whither thou goest.

JEREMIAH 45:2–5

IN the first place we may make a few remarks about Baruch, the person who is addressed by the Lord. In the second place, we shall consider Baruch's complaint: 'Woe is me now! for the LORD hath added grief to my sorrow; I fainted in my sighing, and I find no rest.' And in the third place we shall examine the Lord's dealings with Baruch.

1. Baruch

Baruch, the son of Neriah, was a Jewish prince. He was a godly young man who was deeply devoted to the prophet Jeremiah. He gave every evidence of being gifted and well educated. He acted as the scribe or secretary of Jeremiah by copying out the prophecies which he received from the Lord, although Jeremiah was prophesying for about twenty years before Baruch became his scribe or secretary.

The first mention we have of Baruch is in chapter 32. At that time Jeremiah was a prisoner in the court of the prison, and the word of the Lord came to him. The Lord revealed to him that his uncle's son, Hanameel, would come to him to the court of the prison, requesting that Jeremiah would buy a field for him in Anathoth. 'So Hanameel mine uncle's son came to me in the court of the prison according to the word of the LORD, and said unto me, Buy my field, I pray thee, that is in Anathoth, which is in the country of Benjamin: for the right of inheritance is thine, and the redemption is thine; buy it for thyself. Then I knew that this was the word of the LORD' (Jeremiah 32:8). This was a proof to him that the message he had received was from the Lord: it was confirmed in its fulfilment.

Anathoth was the birthplace of Jeremiah. It is a small town about three miles out of Jerusalem. His cousin reminds him that as a person nigh of kin to him, Jeremiah had the right of redemption. He was duty-bound according to the law to buy the field, otherwise this field would be sold and pass out of the family's possession. We see that Jeremiah acted the part of a kinsman-redeemer in buying the field for his cousin. He gave the two copies of the evidence of the purchase to Baruch. Both the open evidence and the sealed evidence of this transaction were entrusted to Baruch. He was to take these two copies as evidence of the purchase, and put them in an earthen vessel, 'that they may continue many days'.

Matthew Henry suggests that the earthen vessel containing the documentary evidences of the sale was hidden in the field, to remain there for many days—that is, throughout the captivity, as the chapter goes on to show. 'For thus saith the LORD of hosts, the God of Israel; houses and fields and vineyards shall be possessed again in this land' (Jeremiah 32:15). On their return from the captivity, Hanameel or his family could then claim the land as their own. This transaction has a prophetic significance, as the Lord makes clear to the prophet. It was a proof that houses and fields and vineyards would indeed be possessed again in this land after they returned from the captivity.

This transaction also has a spiritual significance. The prophet Jeremiah lived in a cloudy and dark day, a day of blasphemy and rebuke, a day of apostasy from the truth. When solemn judgments on the land were impending, this field was purchased and these evidences were deposited there in an earthen vessel. Spiritually, we may take that to signify how the Lord will preserve his cause. He will have a field, a vineyard of his own purchasing and of his planting, in which he will hide the law and the testimony. Although the multitude will be indifferent to the treasure deposited in the field, the Lord will have his eye on that field, and there will be those who have an interest in that field and in the law and testimony deposited therein until the time come when the Lord shall arise to have mercy upon his Zion.

This transaction was to be a proof—a tangible proof, a prophetic proof—that houses and fields and vineyards were to be possessed again in this land. And it should be an encouragement in a cloudy and dark day that the Lord has his cause in the world, however small it may be. He has a field, and in that field you will find the law and the testimony, and that is proof that he will not forsake his cause. As surely as the Lord returned in mercy to Judah and Jerusalem, and there was again peace and prosperity in the land after the desolations that followed the invasion of Nebuchadnezzar and the captivity, so surely shall the Lord return and build up his cause. We should not therefore despise the day of small things.

After Jeremiah had delivered the evidences of the purchase over to Baruch, he prayed (Jeremiah 32:17–25). In his prayer he is laying hold by faith on the power of the Lord: 'There is nothing too hard for thee.' He was able to turn the captivity of his people and to raise up the desolations of the land.

The next reference to Baruch is in chapter 36, where we find him writing out the prophecies which the prophet received from the Lord. Jeremiah was prevented by the king from prophesying in the temple because he was prophesying of the judgments that were to come. That infuriated the king. But Jeremiah sends Baruch with the prophecy which Baruch copied out from the mouth of Jeremiah, to read it in the house of the Lord (Jeremiah 36:4–8). Then we learn that the princes heard of the solemn warnings that Baruch had read in the temple, and sent for him (verses 14–19).

After that we find the princes reading the roll before the king. So incensed was King Jehoiakim that he cut up the roll and cast it into the fire, giving orders that Jeremiah and Baruch be arrested. But we read in verse 26 how they escaped: 'The LORD hid them.' All the efforts of the men who were sent to arrest them were in vain. And Jeremiah took another roll and gave it to Baruch, 'who wrote therein from the mouth of Jeremiah all the words of the book which Jehoiakim king of Judah had burned in the fire: and there were added besides unto them many like words' (Jeremiah 36:32).

The next reference to Baruch is after the invasion, and after the Jews had been taken captive to Babylon (chapter 42). Many of those who remained in the land decided to go to Egypt, believing it was better for them not to remain in Judah. They made this known to Jeremiah, fully expecting the prophet to support them. But he told them, 'The LORD hath said concerning you, O ye remnant of Judah; Go ye not into Egypt: know certainly that I have admonished you this day' (Jeremiah 42:19). They were not to go into Egypt, and if they did, 'now therefore know certainly that ye shall die by the sword, by the famine, and by the pestilence, in the place whither ye desire to go and to sojourn' (Jeremiah 42:22).

When Jeremiah made this known to the leaders of the remnant that was in the land, they said, 'Oh, these are Baruch's ideas, it's Baruch that's influencing you.' That was how they responded. 'Thou speakest falsely: the LORD our God hath not sent thee to say, Go not into Egypt to sojourn there: but Baruch the son of Neriah setteth thee on against us, for to deliver us into the hand of the Chaldeans, that they might put us to death, and carry us away captives into Babylon' (Jeremiah 43:2–3). These princes, who were the leaders of the remnant, were of the opinion that Baruch was having an influence over the prophet that was not for good, and that when Jeremiah was declaring the mind of the Lord—that they should not go down into Egypt—that Baruch was leading him to prophesy against them.

2. Baruch's complaint

Now we come, in the second place, to make a few remarks about Baruch's complaint. 'Woe is me now! for the LORD hath added grief to my sorrow; I fainted in my sighing, and I find no rest.'

Baruch feels he has trouble upon trouble. He is crushed by his burden of sorrow. 'I am getting no rest from the sorrow that I have. I do not know anyone else who has this particular problem that I have. I seek rest but my sorrow returns.'

We see that the Lord knew about his sorrow. To all appearances, he did not make known his sorrow to the prophet, although he was such a devoted friend, the prophet's secretary, and the one in whom Jeremiah had implicit confidence. It's the Lord who made known to Jeremiah the sorrow that Baruch was expressing in secret. The Lord was hearing his complaint.

The Lord sent a message through the prophet to Baruch regarding his sorrow and trial. In addressing Baruch in the Lord's name, Jeremiah uses the title, 'the God of Israel'. He is speaking to him in the name of the covenant God of Israel, for Baruch was a child of the covenant, and the sorrow and grief that he had at this time were in the covenant for him. The covenant is ordered in all things and sure, and nothing happens by chance to the heirs of promise. Their trials and their sorrows and their griefs are all appointed for them, for the good of their souls. The Lord is here indicating that this was in the covenant for Baruch, although he was so cast down by the sorrow that was causing him to faint and to find no rest. He gives expression to this mournful cry, 'Woe is me now!' as if he had come to the end of all his resources, as if there was no rest or respite for him from the trouble or trial which, to all appearances, he must have had for some time. He had a trial of some kind which was a cause of sorrow to him, and now he says, 'The LORD hath added grief to my sorrow.' He has been praying to the Lord for deliverance, for rest, but he was not getting the deliverance that he was seeking. 'I find no rest.'

Now the Lord opens up why Baruch had this sorrow, and how he was to get rest from it. 'Seekest thou great things for thyself? seek them not,' the Lord says. Dr Gill in his commentary quotes from ancient Jewish rabbis who used to make comments on the Scriptures. Their opinion (which Dr Gill shared) was that among the great things which Baruch sought was that he too would be a prophet of the Lord. He was not receiving the spirit of prophecy as his master Jeremiah received. These rabbis also comment that Joshua, who was so devoted to Moses, was raised up to take the place of Moses. And you have Elisha, who was so devoted to Elijah, raised up to take his place when he was taken away and to become a prophet of the Lord. It would appear that Baruch expected that he too would be raised up as a prophet. He was commissioned by Jeremiah to read publicly these prophecies in the temple before the people, and then before the princes, and then before the king. The position which he held, or the place that Jeremiah was giving him, evidently led Baruch to conclude that he too would be a prophet, and to seek for this. He was not receiving what he sought, the 'great things', and this was the cause of his sorrow and grief, and of his finding no rest in connection with the trouble that was agitating his mind and his soul. He would expect to get rest from it, but back it would come like a flood into his mind, and he would find no rest.

Now the Lord says to him, 'Seekest thou great things for thyself? seek them not.' 'These things are not put out for you. This is how you will find rest in connection with your sorrow, which makes you so cast down in your soul. This is how you will find rest and deliverance: "Seek them not."' He puts a question to Baruch, 'Seekest thou great things for thy thyself?' He had no real warrant to seek for them, for if he had a true warrant from the Lord to seek these things, then the Lord would open up the way for him and encourage him concerning his call to be a prophet of the Lord. But clearly Baruch came to his conclusion because of the position he held and the place that the prophet was giving him. He was copying out the prophecies of Jeremiah and reading them publicly in the temple before the princes and the king. Surely when he was so privileged and so honoured in the house of God, the mantle of prophecy would fall upon him. Just as Joshua and Elisha were raised up to take their masters' places, so Baruch expected this to take place in his own case.

But the Lord makes known to him the judgments that he is to bring upon the land: that which he has built he will break down. That is to say, the temple which had been built as a house for him, and the vineyard which he had planted—the Jewish state—was to be plucked up, even this whole land. God was to bring evil upon all flesh, that is, upon all the people of Judah and Jerusalem.

Baruch may have been expecting other great things too. That is the opinion of the Jewish rabbis whom Dr Gill quotes. He may well have expected to have a position of influence in the kingdom, seeing he was a prince himself and he moved in these circles, and he read the prophecy of Jeremiah at that particular time in the temple, and also before the princes and the king. Perhaps he expected a position of honour, and this was what his heart was set on. And because he was not receiving what he expected to get, this was the cause of his sorrow. But in connection with all the trials and calamities that were to befall Judah and Jerusalem, this was to be Baruch's comfort—the Lord gave him this: 'Thy life will I give unto thee for a prey in all places whither thou goest.' This was to be his staff and stay in the midst of all the calamities and the dangers that would overtake the people of Judah and Jerusalem. He could rest assured of this, that however near death he might come, whatever dangers he might be exposed to, 'thy life will I give unto thee for a prey'.

However near death he might come, his life would be spared till the Lord's appointed time, the time of the covenant. 'A thousand at thy side shall fall, / on thy right hand shall lie / ten thousand dead; yet unto thee / it shall not once come nigh' (Psalm 91:7). 'You will go through them all, and I will preserve your life. Whatever dangers you may be exposed to, you can take this as your staff and your stay, that I will preserve your life.' His natural life, and his soul too, would be preserved at death. That is in the covenant for his people. They will get what is in the covenant for them. The Lord knows what may be the sighs and the cries of his people, what may be casting them down. The Lord knew what was casting down Baruch, and he showed how he could give rest and deliverance. He could have rest by not seeking what he had set his mind on.

'Seekest thou great things for thyself? seek them not.' Amidst all the calamities and dangers through which he would pass in connection with the invasion, his life would be spared. Baruch could therefore say about his troubles, 'It was good for me that I was afflicted—that I went through all that trouble, when I got such an assurance from the Lord and he spoke to me as the covenant God of Israel. He made known that he knows my trial and my sorrows. They were put out for me in the covenant, and I got this promise, 'Thy life will I give unto thee for a prey in all places whither thou goest.'

May he bless his Truth.

The Good Samaritan

But a certain Samaritan, as he journeyed, came where he was: and when he saw him, he had compassion on him, and went to him, and bound up his wounds, pouring in oil and wine, and set him on his own beast, and brought him to an inn, and took care of him. And on the morrow when he departed, he took out two pence, and gave them to the host, and said unto him, Take care of him; and whatsoever thou spendest more, when I come again, I will repay thee.

LUKE 10:33–35

CHRIST spoke the parable of the Good Samaritan in answer to one of the questions that the lawyer put to him. We read that 'a certain lawyer stood up, and tempted him, saying, Master, what shall I do to inherit eternal life?' When we speak of a lawyer we usually think of a person who is trained to administer civil law, but the lawyer in the Scriptures is one who taught the law of Moses and expounded the law of Moses. Gamaliel was a lawyer, a teacher of the law. Nicodemus was a teacher of the law—a teacher in Israel. And the lawyer here was one who taught the law. He put his question in order to tempt the Lord. He thought that he was so learned in the law that he could catch out Christ, and entrap him in his words. It was not because he was exercised with this momentous question, as the Philippian jailer was, and as they were in the day of Pentecost. It was to tempt the Lord that he put this question.

Christ's response was to refer him to the law. 'He said unto him, What is written in the law? how readest thou?' Christ sends proud sinners to the law, that they may see how far short they come of the law; that they may learn experimentally that by the works of the law no flesh can be justified in God's sight.

'And he answering said, Thou shalt love the Lord thy God with all thy heart, and with all thy soul, and with all thy strength, and with all thy mind; and thy neighbour as thyself. And he said unto him, Thou hast answered right; this do, and thou shalt live.'

But as it was not because he was exercised in his soul that he asked this momentous question, the lawyer was not satisfied. The lawyer, 'willing to justify himself, said unto Jesus, And who is my neighbour?' Then we have the parable which Christ spake here, the parable of the Good Samaritan.

In this parable the Lord brought the light of the Truth to bear upon the life of this lawyer. This man had the knowledge in his head of what the law required, but he was not practising what he professed to know and what he professed to teach.

The whole searchlight of the Truth is brought to bear upon the life of the lawyer in this parable. Christ spoke also of the priests and the Levites, how they did not show compassion or give help to the man who had fallen among thieves and was left half-dead by the roadside. They passed by on the other side. The priests and Levites belonged to the same religious class as the lawyer. They too were teachers of the law, and when Christ spoke of the priest and the Levite passing by, no doubt the lawyer could see that his own heart was being set before him in the looking-glass of this parable.

The priest and the Levite showed no compassion to this poor man: they passed him by. That was true of the Pharisees and lawyers, the religious teachers in Christ's day—covetousness was their prevailing sin. The priest and the Levite in the parable were so self-centred and selfish that they would not turn aside from their own hard-beaten path of self-interest to show compassion or to do good to the poor and needy. Christ in this parable was bringing before the lawyer what was true of the religious teachers as a body—how far short they were coming of observing the second table of the law, man's duty to his neighbour. The lawyer answered Christ correctly with the summary of the law, 'Thou shalt love the Lord thy God with all thy heart, and with all thy soul, and with all thy strength, and with all thy mind.' That is the first table of the law. And the second table of the law is summarised as love to our neighbour. But Christ brought the light of Truth to bear upon the conduct of the religious teachers. He was showing the religious teachers of the time their want of compassion, and how far short they came in giving obedience to the second table of the law. They lived for themselves. We often read of Christ warning against covetousness, and how it was the prevailing sin of these people. They were teachers in the synagogue and rulers in the church for filthy lucre's sake. They would not turn aside to give help and compassion to the poor and the needy.

Christ brought before this proud lawyer that aspect of his character. He thought that he could ensnare the Lord by the questions he put. Christ brought before him how far short he came of fulfilling the second table of the law.

Christ also, we believe, in the parable, revealed to these religious teachers how far short they came with respect to the first table of the law. It is implied in this parable, and in the following chapter he says openly, 'Woe unto you, lawyers! for ye have taken the key of knowledge; ye entered not in yourselves, and them that were entering in ye hindered' (Luke 11:52). These teachers professed to have the key of knowledge and to be expounding the law of Moses and the Old Testament Scriptures to the people, but if they had truly had the key of knowledge, they would have seen that the types and prophecies of the Old Testament were being fulfilled in Jesus of Nazareth, that he was the promised Messiah. The predictions as to his birthplace and the tribe from which he would spring, and even the time of his birth, according to the dates given in the prophecy of Daniel and other prophecies all pointed to this glorious truth. If these teachers had been opening up the Scriptures to the people in truth, they would have been leading them into the New Testament church, into the kingdom, leading them to Christ as the promised Messiah. But they were found wanting, not only as to the second table of the law, for they displayed want of love and compassion to their neighbour, but also to the first table.

With respect to the first table of the law, they had taken away the key of knowledge. Their duty to the Lord was to lead sinners into the kingdom by opening up the Scriptures to them. Instead, they sought to prejudice the minds of the people against the Saviour. They taught that salvation was by the works of the law. They themselves went about to establish their own righteousness, and that was the doctrine and teaching that they had for the people. If they were very punctilious in their observances of the ceremonial law and so on, all would be well with them. They taught salvation by works and not by grace. They had taken away the key of knowledge. 'Ye entered not in yourselves.' They did not enter into the kingdom of grace, 'and them that were entering in ye hindered'.

They did not have what the Good Samaritan had for this poor man. The priest and the Levite passed by on the other side. They showed no compassion. But although this stranger did not make such a profession as they did of keeping to the law of Moses, nevertheless he showed that he had love to his neighbour. 'When he saw him, he had compassion on him.' He dismounted from his beast, and went to where the man was, and 'bound up his wounds, pouring in oil and wine'. He did not say to himself, 'Well, I must be prudent. I'll not waste good oil and wine on a total stranger. I shall be in need of it myself.' No, the nature of compassion is to give relief, and this Samaritan showed how he had compassion in his heart toward this poor man. Instead of making excuses why he should keep for himself the oil and the wine which he had, he used them for the wounds of this poor man. And he did not leave him there. He did not say, 'Well, I've made you a bit comfortable now, and somebody else may give you a lift home.' No, he put him on his own beast and brought him to an inn, and took care of him, and paid for his board and keep. How this man showed his compassion!

Christ now puts this question to the lawyer. 'Which now of these three, thinkest thou, was neighbour unto him that fell among the thieves? And he said, He that shewed mercy on him. Then said Jesus unto him, Go, and do thou likewise.'

His message to him was, 'You are maintaining to know and teach what is implied in the second table of the law— love to your neighbour. You have answered rightly all the questions I have put to you. But with all the knowledge you have in your head, you have not put it into practice.' Christ brought the light of this parable to bear upon the life of the lawyer. He was not practising what he knew and what he preached. He says to him now, 'Go and do thou likewise. Do not carry on like the priests and the Levites, but turn aside and do likewise to the poor and needy.'

Then, as I have mentioned, Christ brings the light of this parable to bear on the conduct of the religious teachers of his day, not only with respect to the second table of the law, but also with respect to their shortcomings regarding the first table of the law. Instead of opening up the Scriptures to the people with the key of knowledge, they were prejudicing the minds of the people against Jesus of Nazareth and preaching salvation by works. He pronounces woe upon all who professed to teach the law of Moses and were teachers in the church: they were a stumbling-block to other people who were seeking to enter into the kingdom.

That same woe rests upon religious teachers in every age and generation who do not seek to live according to the pattern Christ sets forth in this parable, those who do not have compassion toward their fellows and toward their neighbour, who do not have love toward God and his Truth, and have taken away the key of knowledge so that they are a stumbling block to those they teach. They teach them salvation by works and not the everlasting gospel. They do not have the oil and wine to meet the case of poor perishing sinners. They do not have the key of knowledge, and thus Christ shows that they were quite unfit for the positions they profess to hold in the church.

But then the parable brings before us that Christ Jesus came to seek and to save that which was lost. This poor man who was left by the wayside half-dead brings before us the condition in which all mankind are as a result of the fall. We are not told why this man went down from Jerusalem to Jericho. He must have thought his journey would be to his advantage and to his profit. Perhaps he never once thought that he would be involved in such a loss—the loss of all that he possessed, and almost the loss of his own life. Our first parents believed the lie of the devil before the Truth of God. They thought they would be as gods, knowing good and evil. But it was going down they were, by acting upon the advice which the enemy gave them, and partaking of the forbidden fruit. Man fell from the estate in which he was created, into an estate of sin and misery.

The thieves stripped this man of his raiment, but in the fall man lost the robe of his original righteousness. He lost the image of God. He lost God, and is in this miserable, deplorable condition. He is dead spiritually, dead in trespasses and in sins. But he is still in the room of mercy. He is still on mercy's ground.

It is more than likely that the traveller in the parable would be unconscious for some time after receiving such cruel handling. It was when he came to that he began to look for help. He looked first of all to the priest and to the Levite—to the religious teachers of the day—so that he might get from them what might meet his condition. But they passed by on the other side. They did not have what would meet his case. They never entered into the kingdom themselves, and those that were entering in they hindered. They had nothing for a poor sinner. They could not understand his condition. They never entered into the kingdom of grace. They never found themselves in this condition—lost and perishing, on the brink of a lost eternity. They knew nothing of the wine and the oil with which the Good Samaritan bound up the wounds of this man.

There is something similar in the parable of the prodigal son. When he had spent his all on riotous living, he went and joined himself to a citizen of that country. That man sent him to feed swine, and he would fain have filled his belly with the husks which the swine ate, but no man gave unto him. It is Dr Gill's opinion that the citizen to whom he joined himself after he left the riotous living was a graceless minister. He had only husks to offer, and the poor prodigal knew no better, but would have filled his belly with the swinish husks. There were persons—ministers, too—who would make a good meal of these husks, but there was nothing in these husks for a poor sinner seeking the bread of life and seeking his way back to the father's house. That citizen was just like the scribes and lawyers, and the priests and the Levites. They had nothing but the husks. They did not have the wine and the oil. They did not enter the kingdom themselves. They took away the key of knowledge. Whatever knowledge they had, they were but darkening counsel with words without knowledge and putting sinners astray for eternity. Although they were so learned in their own estimation, they never entered into the kingdom. Instead of opening up the Scriptures with the key of knowledge, they were just turning people away from the Truth.

That is what is true in our day. Persons may be Bachelors of Divinity and Doctors of Divinity, without having the key of knowledge to enter into the Truth. They never entered in themselves, and how then can they preach the everlasting gospel of our Lord and Saviour Jesus Christ— the gospel of the kingdom? They have nothing but the husks. Whatever scholastic attainments they may have, they have just the husks, not the wine and the oil that will refresh the souls of the poor and the needy. They hinder those who are seeking to enter in, and who seek the way to Zion. They are stumbling blocks to them. When the prodigal son was seeking the way back to the father's house and had come to a knowledge of himself—to a consciousness of his condition as lost sinner, and seeking the provision that was in the father's house—he expected to obtain from this citizen what would meet his needs. 'And he would fain have filled his belly with the husks that the swine did eat.' 'There is a generation that are pure in their own eyes, yet is not washed from their filth-iness' (Proverbs 30:12). They were just self-righteous people. The Saviour adjures his disciples, 'Cast not your pearls before swine.' The swine are people who know nothing of the gracious experience of the Lord's people.

But the pearls are to be opened up to those who fear the Lord. As the Psalmist says, 'All that fear God, come, hear, I'll tell / what he did for my soul' (Psalm 66:16).

The swine are representative of people who are religious in their own estimation, but strangers to grace and to God. The poor prodigal found himself among such. They were making a good meal of the husks. But the prodigal came to realise that he was dying of starvation. It was imperative that he leave that citizen and leave his service. He had to give up his position. He was appointed to feed the swine, but there was nothing for the poor prodigal till he found his way to the father's house.

And this poor traveller of our parable, when he came to himself, naturally looked for support to those who were teachers in the church—the priests und the Levites. But he discovered that they had nothing for him. They passed him by. They would pass him by in their preaching—they could not draw nigh in their preaching to his case, for they had never had faith of their own. They passed him by, and he probably thought there was nothing for him.

We can also take the priest and the Levite to signify the law itself. The sinner who comes to a consciousness of his condition as being a lost sinner who will perish eternally, unless he is delivered from that condition, looks to his own works and to his own resolutions to begin with. But every person whom the Lord visits with his salvation and who is saved by grace, comes to know that there is nothing in the law for him. The law will leave him in that condition—in that lost condition. But the traveller in the parable was brought to know what the Psalmist confessed. 'I look'd on my right hand, and view'd, / but none to know me were; / all refuge failed me, no man / did for my soul take care' (Psalm 142:4).

It was then, when there was no refuge in himself or in any other man, that the Good Samaritan appeared. That is true spiritually. It is when the sinner is brought to the end of his own resources and sees himself lost, and that he has nothing, that Christ appears as the Good Samaritan. The Samaritan came riding on his own beast, and Christ, we may say, comes riding on the white horse of the everlasting gospel. In Revelation Christ comes forth on a white horse, conquering and to conquer—conquering sinners and bringing them into subjection to himself, making them willing in a day of his power through the everlasting gospel. And when the gospel is preached and Christ is going forth, his people will be praying, 'Thine arrows sharply pierce the heart / of th' en'mies of the King; / and under thy subjection / the people down do bring' (Psalm 45:5). They are hoping that the gospel will be blessed to the eternal salvation of sinners.

In the parable, the Good Samaritan lifted the poor man in the condition in which he was, and put him sitting on the beast on which he himself had been riding. Spiritually, sinners come to rest on Christ and his righteousness. He is 'the Lord our righteousness', the one who magnified the law and made it honourable, for apart from having wrought out an everlasting righteousness by his obedience unto death (speaking with all reverence), Christ could not come near any sinner. There would be nothing for sinners but a fearful looking for of judgment and fiery indignation which shall devour the adversary. It is because Christ wrought out an everlasting righteousness that God draws nigh in Christ. God is reconciled in Christ and thus can draw nigh to the sinner. And the sinner is brought to see that he has no righteousness of his own. The poor traveller came to an awareness of his condition. He saw that he was stripped of his raiment, and that he had been robbed of all that he had. He had nothing. He could see his wounds, he could see his blood flowing, and he fully believed his condition would end in death unless someone came to his relief. Then he discovered that there was no relief for him in the priest or the Levite—in the law—in anything he could do himself. It was then that the Good Samaritan appeared. Thus does Christ draw nigh in the everlasting gospel.

The Samaritan bound up the wounds and poured in oil and wine. Oil and wine represent the refreshment and the satisfaction and the reviving that the sinner gets in Christ. He is lifted up out of the fearful pit in which he finds himself, and now he rests upon Christ alone. He rests upon Christ and his righteousness, and not on his own strength or his own righteousness. And in the day that Christ draws nigh, and pours the oil and the wine of his gracious presence into his wounded soul, the poor sinner is lifted up and comes to rest on Christ alone for salvation. 'Those that are broken in their heart, / and grieved in their minds, / he healeth, and their painful wounds / he tenderly upbinds' (Psalm 147:3).

The Good Samaritan did not leave this man there. He took him to an inn, and saw to it that care was taken of him in this inn. The inn in the parable is sometimes explained as being the church of God. The soul is taken to the church. We read that the Lord added to the church 'such as should be saved'. Those who were saved became members in the church. They were brought to a place where they would have their souls fed.

An inn is a place of lodgement; it is not the home. And the church on earth is not the home of his people, those whom the Lord delivers and who have a good hope through grace. He thought upon them in their low estate, and they are now resting upon him. They are coming up out of the wilderness, leaning upon their Beloved. The church on earth is not their home. Their home—their rest—awaits them. 'There remaineth therefore a rest to the people of God' (Hebrews 4:9).

The innkeeper has been taken to be a representation of the ministers of the gospel, who are commissioned to feed the lambs and the sheep. The traveller had been looking to the priest and the Levite, but they had nothing. They passed him by. They had nothing for him, just like the citizen of the far country had nothing for the prodigal. The prodigal discovered that that man had nothing for him but husks, and the living soul will not live upon husks. Swine will feed on husks, but the living soul will turn away from all such food.

When there is famine in the land—not a famine of bread or of water, but of hearing the Word of the Lord—in that day, they will travel from north to south and east to west seeking for the Word of the Lord. What they want is to hear the Word of the Lord preached in accordance with the mind of the Holy Spirit, where they can find what will feed their souls and meet their case. They can find the Lord drawing near to their souls through the ministry, when they are low and cast down, and they will get, per-haps, through the ministry oil and wine which revives and strengthens them. They will get an uplift, they will come to believe that Christ is guiding them in a right way, and that they will not die by the wayside.

Oftentimes they are cast down and feel robbed of all that they ever had. For there are thieves that seek to strip the Lord's people and rob them of all their comforts. The thieves are the world, the flesh and the devil. It is not only at the beginning, when they are brought to see themselves as sinners, but at other times also that they feel poor and cast down. It is vain for a poor person in that condition to go to the religious teachers and expect that he will get something to meet his case. They will pass him by. They do not have the oil and the wine. They can go, as the prodigal did, to the citizen of that country, but they will only get husks. We see that in such a day, those who seek the Word of the Lord will go from place to place and will not find what would satisfy them. We read that the youths and the fair virgins shall faint. They shall faint in their souls. But they are looking to the Lord, for he can supply their need. We do not need to confine the parable to the sinner's conversion—Christ drawing near to the soul when he has nothing—for the gracious soul often finds himself in this condition, cast down because of the way. He has often to confess, 'My folly makes it so.'

This man of our parable might say, 'Well, it's my own fault. If I had not taken this journey, I would not have brought it upon myself.' And when people find them-selves in a similar condition, they take the blame to them-selves. But the Lord will lift up his own. We see how he drew near to this man and brought him to the inn, where there was a person who would take care of him. The inn-keeper had this commission from the Good Samaritan,

'Take care of him,' and the Samaritan gave to the inn-keeper what would meet the needs of this poor man. He gave him two pence, and that has been interpreted as the key of knowledge and the key to the kingdom of heaven. 'I give unto you the keys to the kingdom of heaven'—that is, the key of knowledge to open up the Scriptures and the key of discipline to rule in the Church of God.

Whatever sort of rule the scribes and Pharisees and law-yers had, Christ says that they had not the key of knowledge. They had never entered into the kingdom. But the Lord in his goodness led this man to a place where he could be cared for, and the Lord put him in the care of one to whom he had given the two pence.

Christ brought the light of the parable to bear on the shortcomings of these religious leaders. They were found wanting. Christ in this parable is (as it were) writing on the wall, 'TEKEL: thou art weighed in the balances, and art found wanting.' They were found wanting with re-spect to the claims of the second table of the law—their duty to their neighbour. And they were also found want-ing in the balance of the sanctuary with respect to the claims of the Lord as set forth in the first table of the law. They had neither the key of knowledge nor the key of discipline. They had neither the wine nor the oil. This parable was just the balance of the sanctuary.

'Thou art weighed in the balances, and art found wanting' (Daniel 5:27). In the balances of the sanctuary Christ is weighing the teachers of the law—the lawyers, the scribes and the Pharisees—and he is showing how they were wanting in compassion to the poor and to the needy. They would just pass them by. They would just keep on in their own beaten path of self-interest. The problems of others were not their concern. Whatever they had, they had to be prudent and keep it to themselves, not turn aside to help the poor and the needy. This is what Christ taught the lawyer by this parable. He said, 'Go and do thou likewise.' 'Don't you carry on as you have been do-ing, like the priests and the Levites, but turn aside and get down off the high horse of your pride and go down to where the poor and the needy are. Give them what they need. Thereby you will show that you have respect to the second table of the law.'

He is also showing now far short they came in spiritual matters. As far as temporal matters were concerned, they were found wanting, and they were certainly found want-ing as far as spiritual matters were concerned. Although they had a place in the church of God they had not the key of knowledge. And they were preventing others from entering into the kingdom as well. This parable is a bal-ance in which the Lord weighs the professions of men, and what respect they had to his claims as set forth in the two tables of the law.

Jesus said, 'Go, and do thou likewise.' There is teaching here, and it would be good if we would find ourselves as the traveller found himself. Did we ever come to a con-sciousness of our condition as lost and perishing sinners? And were we convinced of sin because we believed not on Christ? And did we realise that, apart from faith in Christ and being found in him, we would perish? That conviction can be wrought in the soul of a person, with no great trials in connection with it: the Spirit of the Lord can shine in the heart of a person and he can be con-vinced of it. All who are his are brought to see that they will be lost apart from Christ, and they hope that the Lord drew nigh to them in the gospel. They hope that the gospel came to them, not in word only, but in power, and in the Holy Ghost, and in much assurance. They were turned from idols to worship and to serve the one living and true God. They got in the gospel what made Christ precious to them, and they are not now resting upon anything of their own. Instead, they seek to rest upon Christ and him crucified as their righteousness, as their sanctification, their redemption, as their all in all.

They rest on him just as the poor man rested upon the beast on which the Good Samaritan placed him. It is true of those, upon whom he thought in their low estate, that they now seek to rest upon Christ alone.

They discover too that they may look to priests and Levites and such persons, and they will find that they have nothing for them. They pass them by. Whatever academic attainments they may have—whatever theological degrees they may have—they will pass them by. They do not have the wine and the oil: they have only the husks. They do not have the key of knowledge, and they never entered into the kingdom themselves. But the Lord will lead those who need teaching and guiding, just as he led the prodigal son, to where he would get what would feed his soul—away from the man with the husks. This poor traveller must have been so cast down, with the religious teachers of his day passing him by. They did not care, supposing he were to die in that condition. But the Lord met his case. His cares were taken up. The Good Samaritan said to the innkeeper, 'Take care of him,' and he gave him what would take care of him. The traveller would see the goodness of the Samaritan. In every respect, when he looked back, he would see the kindness of the Lord in it all. Just so, Joseph could see the kindness of the Lord in all that he went through, when he was exalted to be lord over all the land of Egypt. Looking back, he would see the kindness of the Lord in all that he passed through.

It is true of all whom the Lord remembers, that they will seek to get what will feed their souls and seek to get what will revive their souls: the wine and the oil. These will revive and refresh them on their journey to that city where 'the Lamb which is in the midst of the throne shall feed them, and shall lead them unto living fountains of waters; and God shall wipe away all tears from their eyes' (Revelation 7:17).

One thing is needful

Lord's Day, 13ᵗʰ February 1966

But one thing is needful; and Mary hath chosen that good part, which shall not be taken away from her.

LUKE 10:42

IN verse 38 we read that Christ and his disciples entered into a certain village, and a certain woman named Martha received him into her house. The village was Bethany, and Christ received hospitality in the house of Martha, her sister Mary, and her brother Lazarus. We read that Christ loved Martha and Mary and their brother Lazarus. They were all loved by the Saviour, and they showed their love and devotion to Christ and to his disciples by keeping an open door for them, and entertaining them when they came to Bethany.

When the Lord opens the heart, he opens the house. That was also true in the case of Lydia. When the Lord opened her heart, she opened her house to the disciples of the Lord. That is true still. Where there is an open heart there will be open house and an open purse. As the late Mr

147

Macfarlane said, 'If it is not possible to open the house, the purse will be open.' The confession of those whose hearts been opened is, 'All things come of thee, and of thine own have we given thee' (1 Chronicles 29:14). All that they have is from the Lord, and whatsoever they give the Lord is what the Lord has given them. But where there is not an open purse to the cause of Christ, it is to be greatly feared that the heart was never in truth opened, for it is in the nature of the grace of love to give. As it is the nature of faith to receive, it is the nature of love to give—and to seek to give to the Lord and to his cause and to his people.

We read of Mary that she sat at Jesus' feet. It was not Mary only who sat at Jesus' feet: Martha and Lazarus also sat at Jesus' feet. To sit at someone's feet is a Hebrew expression. It means to be a pupil or disciple. The apostle Paul sat at the feet of Gamaliel: in other words, he received teaching and instruction from him.

That was true of Martha, Mary and Lazarus. They were all disciples of Christ, who sat at his feet and learned of him. But on this particular occasion when Christ was in the house, opening up to them the everlasting gospel, we see that Martha was cumbered about much serving. When Christ began his discourse, Mary left the household duties and sat down at Jesus' feet to hear the gracious words that were proceeding from his mouth. It was not every day she would have such a blessed opportunity of hearing the Saviour preach the everlasting gospel. But Martha, on the other hand, was so troubled about the serving—so much had to be done, so many guests had to be attended on— that she could not see her way to leave the matters that were a concern to her mind, and to sit down. She was in quite a bustle with all that had to be done. She thought it was her duty to attend to those things. She was so confident that she was in the path of duty regarding the serving that she came to the Lord and said to him, 'Lord, dost thou not care that my sister hath left me to serve alone? Bid her therefore that she help me.'

But then we have Christ's answer. 'Martha, Martha, thou art careful and troubled about many things'—things that were lawful and good in themselves. 'But one thing is needful.' *That* thing we are to be supremely concerned with. However lawful and good other matters may be in their own place, they will last but for a season. They will pass away. They constitute but a temporary portion. But this is the one thing needful. This good part shall never be taken from those who make choice of it.

1. In the first place, we may notice a few things about the one thing needful. It is a good part which shall not be taken from those who make choice of it.

2. In the second place we shall notice a few things implied in making choice of the one thing needful.

3. In the third place we shall make a few remarks about the assurance which Mary got at this time—an assurance from the lips of the Saviour that she had made choice of that good part that would not be taken from her.

1. The one thing needful

The Word of God makes clear what that one thing needful is. The one thing needful in view of death and eternity is to have Christ as our portion—our Saviour—to be found in him. 'He that hath the Son hath life; he that hath not the Son of God hath not life' (1 John 5:12). He may have health. He may have wealth. He may have a good home. He may have prospects. He may have worldly success. He may have all his heart's desire, all that this world can give him. But he that hath not the Son of God hath not life. He does not have the one thing needful. He is without God and without hope in the world. What a sad state for a person to be in! Engrossed in the world, and encumbered and taken up with the world and its ways, lawful though many things are in themselves. Expecting success and all worldly happiness and worldly prosperity. Yet across his life and all that he has, the Holy Spirit writes these solemn words: 'Without God and without hope in the world!'

Christ is declaring to us in the gospel the one thing needful. However encumbered we may be with things which are lawful and good in themselves, it is to this one thing that our attention is called by the Lord in his Truth. How solemn the thought, if we die without the one thing needful! This is the only preparation that will stand us for death and for eternity, to have Christ as the portion of our souls, and be enabled to say, 'The LORD is my portion, saith my soul; therefore will I hope in him' (Lamentations 3:24).

How solemn if death finds us without the one thing needful! How many there are to whom death comes unexpectedly—to young and old and middle-aged! And it is to be feared in the case of many that they go to eternity without the one thing needful. Death will put a separation between us and all that we may have now, all that we were setting our hearts upon, and that we think so much of and see as so needful! When death comes, we must part

with it all. And the Lord who is yet to be our judge is
here saying to us, 'One thing is needful.' He says also,
'What shall it profit a man, if he shall gain the whole
world, and lose his own soul? Or what shall a man give in
exchange for his soul?' (Mark 8:36–37).

We are in danger of dying without the one thing needful.
We can be so engrossed by the lawful things—by our daily concerns—that we neglect the one thing needful. The
rich man who prospered in this world said he would pull
down his barns and build greater. He said to his soul,
'Soul, thou hast much goods laid up for many years.' He
had a good bank account, he had prospered well on his
farm, and he was now going to retire. He had much laid
up for many years. 'Now, take thine ease; eat, drink and
be merry. Enjoy your leisure time now.' He was promising himself many years. He must have been a pretty
healthy man. To all appearances he would live many years
yet. But the Lord said, 'Thou fool, this night shall thy soul
be required of thee.' He was a fool spiritually. However
wise he was in connection with his worldly concerns, he
was a fool as far as the salvation of his soul and the one
thing needful were concerned. What a night it was for
that poor man when his soul plunged into outer darkness!
He died in his sins. He died in despair.

And that is our danger. We know not what a day nor an
hour may bring forth. And these solemn words come to
us, to warn of the uncertainty of our time. We may be
promising ourselves many things, like this rich man, but it
is what the Lord says that shall stand. Therefore we are
called upon to prepare ourselves. 'Prepare to meet thy
God, O Israel' (Amos 4:12). 'Thou shalt surely die and
not live.' And the only preparation that will stand us is to

have the one thing needful. Every other thing, however needful and good, will leave us at death. But as Christ says, 'Whoso findeth me findeth life, and shall obtain favour of the LORD' (Proverbs 8:35).

Those who have the one thing needful have what will stand them for eternity. They are a happy people. They alone are a happy people. 'Happy art thou, O Israel; who is like unto thee, O people saved by the LORD, the shield of thy help, and who is the sword of thy excellency! and thine enemies shall be found liars unto thee; and thou shalt tread upon their high places' (Deuteronomy 33:29). They only are a blessed people, whose God is the Lord, who have the Lord as the portion of their souls. Whatever trials and tribulations they may have to endure in this life, they have the promise, 'All things work together for good to them that love God, to them who are the called according to his purpose' (Romans 8:28). When Christ here calls upon us to seek the one thing needful, he calls upon us to seek himself. He is that good part that shall not be taken from those who make choice of him.

We are called upon to seek him. 'Seek ye the LORD while he may be found, call ye upon him while he is near: let the wicked forsake his way, and the unrighteous man his thoughts: and let him return unto the LORD, and he will have mercy upon him; and to our God, for he will abundantly pardon' (Isaiah 55:6–7).

These gracious invitations are extended to us, that we might be found turning to the Lord and not halting, as others were, between two opinions. As the Lord said to Israel through his prophet Elijah, 'How long halt ye between two opinions? if the LORD be God, follow him;

but if Baal, then follow him' (1 Kings 18:21). It is either the Lord or Baal. It is either Christ and the salvation that is in him, or the pleasures of sin which are but for a season. There is one thing needful, and those who make choice of that good part find it to be a portion that shall never be taken from them.

2. Making choice of the one thing needful

We shall in the second place notice a few things implied in the making of this choice. The Lord says to Peter, 'If I wash thee not, thou hast no part with me' (John 13:8). The choice of that good part is the fruit of the washing wherewith Christ washes those who are his people. This washing is 'the washing of regeneration, and renewing of the Holy Ghost' (Titus 3:5). The renewing of the Holy Ghost *is* the washing of regeneration: it is the person being renewed in the spirit of his mind through the gracious and efficacious teaching of the Holy Spirit. This work of the Holy Spirit is variously described as a washing, a renewing and an ingrafting. His gracious work is brought before us in different metaphors in the Scriptures.

This washing—the renewing of the Holy Ghost—is the effectual call of the Holy Spirit. Apart from his effectual call and work, no sinner can come to Christ. Christ himself declares that. 'No man can come to me, except the Father which hath sent me draw him: and I will raise him up at the last day' (John 6:44). The drawing of the Father, as Christ goes on to point out, is the teaching of the Father through the Spirit who is sent by the Father and by the Son. All who are God's children are taught by him. Making this choice of the good part that shall not be taken from us is bound up with the gracious teaching, the effectual work, of the Holy Spirit.

The Holy Spirit's work includes convincing us of sin and of misery, as the Shorter Catechism puts it. The sinner is brought to see that he is a sinner. He is convinced that all he has—however good and lawful his portion in this world—will not stand him for eternity. He is convinced that unless he has Christ as his portion, he shall die in despair, and that his portion in eternity will be with the devil end his angels. These convictions lay hold of the mind of the person who is taught by the Holy Spirit. He might not know at the time that it is the Holy Spirit who is teaching him, but he comes to see the vanity of all that this world can give. And this is brought home to him: 'One thing is needful.'

Now, when the Holy Spirit convinces the Lord's people of sin, he brings some through great terrors of mind. In the case of others, their conviction is deep and calm. Yet in both cases, the sure conviction is wrought in the soul, 'If I die in this condition, I shall perish eternally.' We must not think that the terrors which the Philippian jailer and others experienced are always connected with the convincing work of the Holy Spirit. There is a certain terror of mind, a fear that the person may perish eternally. But a person may be assured of this in his soul without being distracted outwardly. What is necessary in conviction of sin is that the sinner is convinced that apart from being found in Christ and having Christ, he shall perish eternally—whatever he may have, whatever knowledge he may have, however circumspect he may be and whatever good things he may have in this life. He has that conviction, and nothing will meet the need he now feels in his soul except Christ, the one thing needful. Nothing that this world or any finite creature can give him can meet that need. He may get friendship from the Lord's people, he may get sympathy from them, and counsel, and so on, but whatever they may seek to give, the poor sinner is conscious of this need—he is still without God and without hope in the world.

In the work of effectual calling, the Holy Spirit also enlightens the mind in the knowledge of Christ. We may have great knowledge about Christ, and yet not know Christ. Persons who are of a religious turn of mind can write books about Christ, and they can even preach about Christ. They can devote themselves to theology and be orthodox, and so on, and yet not know Christ. But in effectual calling the sinner is both brought to the conviction that he does not know Christ, and he is enlightened in the knowledge of Christ. We need divine illumination—light from heaven—to bring us to a saving knowledge of the Lord Jesus Christ.

The soul is enlightened in the knowledge of Christ through the Truth. The soul is made able and willing to close in with Christ and to receive Christ as he is freely offered in the gospel. The soul closes in with Christ, for Christ is revealed to the soul. The soul and Christ meet, however short the meeting may seem to be. The soul goes forth, as it were, out of itself, to the Lord and rests on the Lord. That puts a distinction between the person who is self-deceived through his knowledge and an outward change in behaviour, and the true believer who is brought to a knowledge of Christ.

And in the day in which the soul closes in with Christ and receives Christ, he is from that day forward a disciple of Christ, one who sits at the feet of Christ and who is seeking to learn of Christ. We see that in the case of the man out of whom the Lord cast the legion of devils. Once Satan was cast out and the Lord took possession of his soul, we read that he sat at the feet of Christ, clothed and in his right mind. He sat at Christ's feet literally, and it was true of him spiritually as well. He was now learning from this person who had delivered him from the power of darkness and translated him into his own kingdom.

Those who have made this choice are sitting at the feet of Christ. They seek to learn of him. And what is it that they are seeking to learn? What is the exercise of the souls of those who have made this choice? Well, the exercise which the apostle had (and he speaks on behalf of the church of God) is, 'that I might be found in him, not having mine own righteousness, which is of the law, but that which is through the faith of Christ, the righteousness which is of God by faith' (Philippians 3:9). Paul's desire was to be in Christ, and yet he already was in Christ. It is those who are in Christ who seek to be found in Christ. Likewise, it is those who have been called effectually who seek to make their calling and election sure. It is those who have been taught by Christ who seek to learn of him. They desire to make sure that what they hope they got was the real thing, that they are not deceiving themselves and deceiving others. They are exercised regarding this momentous matter.

Unbelief and Satan wax against grace, and seek to blind and overthrow them. But whatever they have to endure, and however downcast they may be, the characteristic of those who have been called effectually is that the bent and bias of their soul is toward Christ. They desire that they would be clothed upon with his righteousness and that they would be cleansed from sin. In the days when there were sailing vessels, a ship might be sailing westwards and then a blast of wind might come and send it in the opposite direction. But when the wind calmed and the sailors once more took control of the sails, the ship would be turned round to face the correct direction. The same may be true of the temptations of Satan and the flesh and the world. The Lord's people may be turned from their course, and they may even believe they are on the wrong course altogether, such is the power of temptation. But once they are delivered from the temptation they make for the desired haven. The language of their souls is, 'To whom shall we go? Thou hast the words of eternal life.'

They seek to learn of him. They are found at his feet. They learn of him as their prophet. God's Word is the revelation of his mind, and is alone able to make them wise unto salvation. They seek to know his mind as that is revealed in the Word of God, and instruction that is contrary to God's Word they cannot receive. 'My sheep hear my voice' (John 10:27). They hear what Christ says in his Truth as the Good Shepherd—the prophet of their souls—and a stranger they will not follow. When someone comes along with strange doctrines and fanciful ideas, persons who have not the root of the matter can be taken aside and bewitched, and embrace what is false. But those who are his people will reject what is contrary to his holy Word.

They are sitting at his feet to learn of him as their priest, for they have experienced that they are sinners. And the longer they live, the more they are brought to know the corruption of their nature and their need of the blood—the precious blood of Christ—that cleanseth from all sin. They cannot cleanse themselves, and it is comfort to them that Christ has made provision for the cleansing of sinners.

They sit at his feet as their king, desiring to submit their will to him and to take his yoke upon them. 'Take my yoke upon you, and learn of me.' That is the yoke of his commandments. They seek to acknowledge him as their Lord and Master, as their King, and to submit to his dealings with them in providence. They seek the grace of submission. They seek to be delivered from a murmuring spirit, which is of the flesh, and they seek to have what is of the Spirit. It was the fruit of the Spirit that the Psalmist had when he said, 'Dumb was I, opening not my mouth, / because this work was thine' (Psalm 39:9). They seek to kiss the rod and him who has appointed it, believing that 'the Lord is just in all his ways, / holy in his works all' (Psalm 145:17). They will seek grace to submit to the Lord in all the dispensations of his providence. In that way they show that they are his disciples.

This choice of Christ and of the gospel is the same choice that Moses made. By faith Moses chose 'rather to suffer affliction with the people of God, than to enjoy the pleasures of sin for a season'. Where there is choice of Christ, there is a choice of his people. 'I am companion to all those / who fear, and thee obey' (Psalm 119:63). The person who has chosen Christ will have new companions. He will have the confession of Ruth: 'Thy people shall be my people, and thy God my God' (Ruth 1:16). He will have respect unto the recompense of the reward. He now has his eyes on eternity and on the reward, which is reckoned not of debt but of grace—the crown of eternal life that the Lord's people receive at death. These are the things that now occupy his soul. He presses toward the mark, toward the prize of the high calling of God in Christ Jesus.

Great efforts are made by Satan, the flesh and the world to rob him of his interest in Christ, to darken his evidences, to cast him down. And at times he will conclude that he never made this choice. But the Lord will not leave his own. And however dejected and downcast they may be, beset by Satan and unbelief, yet when the Lord lifts up the light of his countenance on them, their comforts are re-stored. Then they seek to praise the Lord with the Psalm-ist: 'I love the Lord, because my voice / and prayers he did hear. / I, while I live, will call on him, / who bow'd to me his ear' (Psalm 116:1).

They are a tried and an afflicted people, but their desire is to trust in the name of the Lord. 'The name of the LORD is a strong tower; the righteous runneth into it, and is safe.' They believe there is one thing needful, and it is this they seek during their life's journey. They are not like some who 'choose' Christ und then can fold their arms in complacency. It is a lifelong struggle with the believer— he is in a conflict from which there is no discharge while he is in this life. It is the choice of his soul to follow the Lamb in this world, through good and evil report. He shows by his walk and conversation whose he is and whom he serves.

3. Mary's assurance

In the last place we shall notice the assurance Mary got at this time. Martha was cumbered about much serving. There was much to be done. They were serving the Lord and his disciples, whom they had invited to their home.

It was true of Martha as well as of Mary that she had made choice of that good part that would not be taken from her. And it was also true of Lazarus. They were all loved by the Lord. Moses says in his blessing of the children of Israel, 'Yea, he loved the people; all his saints are in thy hand: and they sat down at thy feet; every one shall receive of thy words' (Deuteronomy 33:3). That is where his people desire to be: at his feet. Their souls are at home there. They say, 'It is good for us to be here.'

These are a people who have been loved by the Lord. It was his love that brought them to this wealthy place. Behind their choice of him is his choice of them and his eternal love of them. 'Ye have not chosen me, but I have chosen you' (John 15:16). 'Yea, I have loved thee with an everlasting love: therefore with lovingkindness have I drawn thee' (Jeremiah 51:3). It is proof of his everlasting love that his people desire to be sitting at his feet and learning of him.

Those who are effectually called are described as saints, and they are in the Lord's hand, and no man shall pluck them out of his hand. This good part shall not be taken from them: it is in the keeping of the Lord. Satan went very far in seeking to take that good part from Peter when he was in Satan's sieve. But the Lord showed clearly that Peter, even when denying his Master with oaths in Satan's sieve, was still in the keeping of the Keeper of Israel, who slumbers not nor sleeps. 'Simon, Simon, behold, Satan hath desired to have you, that he may sift you as wheat; but I have prayed for thee, that thy faith fail not' (Luke 22:31–32). He was in the keeping of Christ, and because he was in Christ's hand, he was brought back to sit at his feet again in his soul's experience.

'Yea, he loved the people.' They will receive from his table what will sustain and uphold them, for Christ has the tongue of the learned, and he is able to speak a word in season to him that is weary. It is one thing to make choice of the good part; it is another to enjoy the assurance Mary received at this time. Martha and Lazarus had made the same choice of the good part, but at this time Martha was so encumbered in her mind about the serving that she could not see her way to leave the serving, to sit down and hear what the Saviour had to say. She believed that her duty was at this time to attend to the serving. She was so certain that she was in the path of duty that she went to Christ and said to him, 'Lord, dost thou not care that my sister hath left me to serve alone? Bid her therefore that she help me.'

This shows that there are times when the Lord's people adopt an attitude or position which they are quite sure is right, and yet they are mistaken. Martha was so sure that she was in the path of duty that she appealed to the Lord himself and to his church—the apostles—expecting that they would justify her and condemn Mary. And no doubt the apostles would have supported her. But the Lord himself settled the matter. Instead of justifying Martha, he rebuked her.

The rebuke was in love. That is evident from the repetition of her name. The very taste of love is in the rebuke. Very often when we give a rebuke, we may do so in a sharpish way, with the result that the rebuke is lost on the person. But this rebuke was not lost on Martha. 'Whom the Lord loveth he chasteneth' (Hebrews 12:6). 'As many as I love, I rebuke and chasten: be zealous therefore, and repent' (Revelation 3:19). He rebukes his own sometimes privately and sometimes publicly. His own works are without rebuke. If a rebuke is not taken, he chastens them.

Martha took the rebuke. Later on, six days before the passover, shortly before Christ's death, Simon the leper made a feast for Christ and his disciples, and we read that Martha was serving. She did not say, 'Well, this is all the thanks I'm getting for all my serving and all my hospitality, and all I've been trying to do: I'm just rebuked for it. This is the end of serving for me.' No! She showed that the Lord's rebuke was blessed to her. Later on, she is found serving, but now she knows how to serve. She does not serve when the Lord is speaking. She puts first things first. She was put right in her mind, to 'seek first the kingdom of God, and his righteousness; and all things shall be added unto you'.

Martha was a good person—a godly person—who was devoted to her Lord and Master, and yet she took this attitude. The incident shows that there was something wrong somewhere. The things that were such a concern to the poor woman and taking such a hold on her mind were a means, not of causing her to sit at Christ's feet, but of separating her from the fellowship that Mary and the apostles were having at that particular time in listening to what the Saviour had to say. This concern about the serving was a means of taking her aside—putting her on her own.

When some concern gets a hold of a gracious person's mind, and is a means of isolating him, not drawing him nearer to the Lord and to his people, there must be something wrong. The person may be sure that he is in the path of duty, that the Lord will uphold him and justify him, and his church too. Yet if it has this fruit, that it comes between that person and the fellowship of the brethren, then there must be something wrong.

Martha was not taking a low place. You can see that by the way she spoke. It was not the spirit of love and power and of a sound mind that was in exercise: the old nature was a bit ruffled in her. She spoke abruptly, peremptorily, even to the Lord. The grace of love was not in exercise in her soul at this time. She was sitting in condemnation on her sister, and she was possessed of a contentious spirit. The whole thing was stirring up the old nature. That is evident in the way she spoke, and in the way she acted—which was a means of putting her apart, alone.

And very often when a person is separate like that, and they're alone, and they are sure in their own estimation that they are right, they develop self-pity. Not only did Martha have a contentious spirit, she was also possessed by self-pity. Such people often have a martyr complex. They feel that everyone is against them, that they are being persecuted. You can see that with Elijah the prophet, great man though he was. The Lord had to rebuke him for it. He thought that he was being persecuted by everybody, and that he was the sole witness for the Truth. And he had to be rebuked for that.

When you see these fruits—persons quite sure that they are right and that the Lord will justify them, and yet it is a means of separating them from the brethren, and they develop this martyred attitude, it is evident there is something wrong. I have known people like this. If you disagreed with them, you were their enemy; if you sympathised with them, you were their friend. They felt themselves so crossed and ill-treated and sorry for themselves. And this was a means of separating them from the fellowship of the brethren, and from having the spirit of love and of power and of a sound mind.

You can see all that in the case of Martha. Although she was so sure of the rightness of her cause, the Lord in his love rebuked her. The Lord will rebuke his own people, as surely as he rebuked the prophet. His loving rebuke brought Martha to her right mind. She could see now how she had gone astray in that particular matter.

In conclusion, it is evident that it may not have been easy for Mary to leave the household duties and sit down to hear what the Saviour had to say. If Martha spoke like that in the presence of the Lord and his disciples about her sister—publicly—one wonders what she said to her in private. To all appearances, the house belonged to Martha. Poor Mary would realize that if she left the serving, she would incur the resentment and anger of her sister. There was so much to be done. But in spite of all these obstacles, she did not keep the peace by staying where she was. No, she saw this to be the one thing needful. This was the path of duty for her—to sit and listen to what the

Saviour was saying. And she got this assurance from the Lord that she had made choice of that good part that would not be taken from her.

When it is not easy for the Lord's people to put first things first, and when there are other things to be done that are so needful and so lawful—and they meet with the resentment of their nearest and dearest, and this mountain and that mountain is before them—and when they nevertheless seek to give Christ the pre-eminence and to sit at his feet, it is then that they can receive the blessing. And I'm sure Mary would say, 'What a blessing that I sat down, that I left everything to avail myself of that opportunity! What a blessing I received!' She got a blessing that she would remember for the rest of her days.

Martha got a blessing too. There is assurance to be had from the fact that it is those whom the Lord loves that he rebukes and chastens. Martha was brought to her right mind. And no doubt she would be quite apologetic to her sister. 'When a man's ways please the LORD, he maketh even his enemies to be at peace with him' (Proverbs 16:7). They would discuss what they had heard: the blessing that Mary got in the assurance she got, and the blessing that Martha got from the rebuke which the Lord so lovingly gave her.

'One thing is needful; and Mary hath chosen that good part, which shall not be taken away from her.'

May he bless his Truth.

The Master is come, and calleth for thee

Lord's Day, 27th March 1966

And when she had so said, she went her way, and called Mary her sister secretly, saying, The Master is come, and calleth for thee.
JOHN 11:28

WE will especially consider the words, 'The Master is come, and calleth for thee.' In the first place we can make a few remarks on the circumstances in which this message was delivered to Mary; in the second place, the name which Martha here gives to Christ; and thirdly, a few things implied in the message itself.

1. The circumstances of the message

In this chapter we have an account of the sickness, death and resurrection of Lazarus. We read how his sisters Martha and Mary were exercised regarding their brother's sickness. We are told that 'Jesus loved Martha, and her sister, and Lazarus'. It is in connection with this trial that Christ's love is here mentioned. For however sore the trial was, it was sent in love. 'Whom the Lord loveth he chasteneth, and scourgeth every son whom he receiveth' (Hebrews 12:6). The trials and chastisements which the Lord gives to his own are tokens of his love as surely as the great and precious promises he gives them.

When Lazarus took sick, his sisters sent word to Jesus saying, 'Lord, behold, he whom thou lovest is sick.' They evidently sent a messenger to the place where Jesus was. The Saviour knew all things, but the sisters were exercised in presenting this petition to the Lord. They were crying to the Lord in the day of their trouble. 'Call upon me in the day of trouble: I will deliver thee, and thou shalt glorify me' (Psalm 50:15). When Jesus heard, he said, 'This sickness is not unto death, but for the glory of God, that the Son of God might be glorified thereby.' This is the answer that Christ gave.

It is clear from what Jesus said to Martha at the grave that this message must have been delivered to the sisters. When their messenger returned they would naturally ask, 'Is Jesus coming? When is he coming?' or 'What did he say?' And the messenger would reply, 'He said, "This sickness is not unto death, but for the glory of God, that the Son of might be glorified thereby."' At the grave Christ reminds Martha of this message. No doubt the sisters had concluded from the Saviour's words that Lazarus would recover. No doubt the promise gave them joy when he said, 'This sickness is not unto death, but for the glory of God, that the Son of might be glorified thereby.'

But Lazarus grew worse instead of recovering and at last he died and was buried. And to all appearances Martha and Mary buried the promise in the grave along with Lazarus. For Lazarus and the promise were so intimately bound together that when he died and was buried, they could not see how the promise could live, how the promise could be fulfilled.

But even if the Lord had not raised Lazarus, this promise *would* have been fulfilled. Even if Lazarus had not been resurrected, this promise would have been for the glory of God.

We find Christ saying, 'Whosoever liveth and believeth in me shall never die.' 'Whosoever liveth'—that is, who has spiritual life in his soul—'and believeth in me'—for it is those whom he has quickened, who believe in him—'*they* shall never die.' Death will be to them but a door of entrance into the fulness of life that is at God's right hand. They never die in the sense that the wicked dies. I have heard of persons who had such a promise in connection with a loved one who was sick and who then died. They were greatly troubled because the promise was not fulfilled literally. But although natural life was not restored, and although the person did not recover from sickness, nevertheless the promise was fulfilled in the higher sense. The Saviour says, 'He shall never die.' For at death his people enter into the fulness of life and fulness of joy that is at God's right hand.

Martha and Mary put their own construction on this promise and believed that Lazarus was to be restored, but we see how their faith was tried in connection with the promise. Before the Lord fulfils any of his promises, as a rule, his people's faith is tried. We see that in the case of Abraham. The Lord promised Abraham that he would have a son by Sarah. No doubt that promise brought joy to both Abraham and Sarah, but we see how their faith was tried. They had to wait for twenty-five years before they saw the fulfilment of the promise. According to the course of nature it was impossible for the promise to be fulfilled, but 'the things which are impossible with men are possible with God' (Luke 18:27), 'for with God all things are possible' (Mark 10:27). When, humanly speaking, it was impossible for Sarah to have a son, we see that the Lord in his own appointed time fulfilled his promise.

In connection with that, we read that Abraham 'was strong in faith, giving glory to God' (Romans 4:20), believing that he who gave the promise was able to fulfil it. The strength of his faith became apparent when he was tried as to the promise. 'Who against hope believed in hope, that he might become the father of many nations, according to that which was spoken, So shall thy seed be. And being not weak in faith, he considered not his own body now dead, when he was about an hundred years old, neither yet the deadness of Sarah's womb: he staggered not at the promise of God through unbelief; but was strong in faith, giving glory to God; and being fully persuaded that, what he had promised, he was able also to perform.' (Romans 4:18–21).

Joseph is another example. The dreams which the Lord gave to Joseph were God's promises to him. But before the Lord fulfilled his word to Joseph, we see how his faith was tried. For the word of the Lord tried him in prison. What trials he went through! It was when matters were at their darkest and when, humanly speaking, it was impossible for such promises to be fulfilled, it was then that the Lord intervened, and raised Joseph from a dungeon in the prison of Egypt to be ruler over all the land .

In the case of this promise which Martha and Mary received concerning their brother, how their faith was tried! How they would have rejoiced in soul when they received the promise, 'This sickness is not unto death, but for the glory of God, that the Son of God might be glorified thereby'! But how everything in providence went contrary to the promise, as it did with Abraham and with Joseph! That is very often the way in which his people's faith will be tried. They will find themselves as Martha did at the grave—with the promise, as it were, buried in the grave. For as we have already remarked, Lazarus and the promise were so intimately bound together that when he died and was buried, his sisters could not see how the promise could be fulfilled and they buried (as it were) the promise in the grave of unbelief.

Very often that is how it is in the experience of his own people, for they have not that strong faith which Abraham had. Although they are duty-bound to give glory to God and to believe that he is able, they often find themselves like Martha. There was Lazarus stinking in the grave, and a gravestone over the grave: it was humanly impossible for the promise to be fulfilled. Similarly, the Lord's people may be conscious of their own corruption within and see a gravestone without—obstacles without and obstacles within. It appears just impossible for the promise to be fulfilled.

It is in such circumstances that the Lord intervenes and manifests forth his glory. As he said to Martha, 'Said I not unto thee, that, if thou wouldest believe, thou shouldest see the glory of God?' And they saw the glory of God. He manifested his power in raising Lazarus from the dead when matters were at their darkest, and when they had buried the promise in the grave of unbelief.

He first of all gave a resurrection to the promise. He quickened her faith in saying to her, 'Said I not unto thee?' There is a rebuke in these words—a rebuke of her unbelief. When the Lord rebukes unbelief he strengthens faith in himself. Then he resurrected Lazarus. Martha was able to exercise faith in him, and it is in connection with exercising faith in him as the resurrection and the life that he manifested forth his glory in restoring Lazarus from the dead.

It was in the darkest circumstances, when to all appearances it was impossible for the promise to be fulfilled, that Mary received this message in her disconsolate and downcast condition, 'The Master is come, and calleth for thee.'

2. The Master

We shall in the second place make a few remarks about the title which Martha here gives to Christ: 'The Master'.

Christ is the one who is in supreme control. He is Master over all things . All things are put under his feet, and he is given to be head over all things to his church, 'the fulness of him that filleth all in all'. All things are under his control in providence and in grace, from the falling of a sparrow to the falling of an empire. His control over all things in providence is so minute and particular that he declares that the very hairs of his people's heads are numbered. Whatever circumstances they find themselves in, however distressing, however trying and dark, he is the Master. He is in control. The waves may lift up their voice and make a mighty noise; his people may be tempest-tossed, as the disciples were in the storm. And Christ may be silent and, as far as they can see, indifferent to their plight. They may say as the disciples said, 'Carest thou not that we perish?' But he showed in his own appointed time that he was master of the situation, that the winds and waves were under his control. However near to shipwreck they were and to perishing, as they themselves concluded, and although he was asleep in the hinder part of the ship—asleep as to his manhood, but awake as to his Godhood—he was all the time in control. And in his own appointed time, he arose and rebuked the winds and the waves, and instantly there was a great calm. He rebuked their unbelief too when he said, 'O ye of little faith,' and called faith into exercise in himself as the one who was in control of the winds and of the waves.

Martha here speaks of him as 'the Master'. Whatever our trying circumstances may be, he is the Master. That was a comfort to Job in his trials. He could say, 'He knoweth the way that I take: when he hath tried me, I shall come forth as gold' (Job 23:10). For the Lord will try his own. He says, 'I will bring the third part through the fire, and will refine them as silver is refined, and will try them as gold is tried: they shall call on my name, and I will hear them: I will say, It is my people: and they shall say, The LORD is my God' (Zechariah 13:9). He will bring them through the fire of the trials and afflictions which he has appointed for them. As he said to the disciples, 'In the world ye shall have tribulation: but be of good cheer; I have overcome the world' (John 16:33).

They are not to be left in the fire. Whatever fires they have to pass through, it is for their spiritual good. He will remove from them their dross and their tin. The trial of their faith is as of gold tried in the fire, and these trials are for their good. He is the Master. He is over Satan and his temptations. He can rebuke the adversary. He 'will not suffer you to be tempted above that ye are able; but will with the temptation also make a way to escape, that ye may be able to bear it' (1 Corinthians 10:13).

He is Master also in his own house. He has all power in heaven and on earth. His purposes shall be fulfilled. He shall bring to nought all the counsels of men and his counsel shall stand. 'O but the counsel of the Lord / doth stand for ever sure; / and of his heart the purposes / from age to age endure' (Psalm 33:11).

We read that Moses as a servant was faithful in his house, that is, the Old Testament church. He was faithful in setting up the Old Testament worship, in erecting the tabernacle, and in doing all things in accordance with the pattern shown him in the mount. Moses was faithful as a servant, but Christ is faithful as a Son, as Lord over his own house. Those who acknowledge him as their Lord and Master, they recognise him, they seek to honour him as Master over his own house. They would seek to know him in submitting to his will in connection with the ruling of his own house and with the worship he requires.

In the days of Malachi, when the visible church had departed far from the Truth, and the people were to a large extent given over to worldliness and ungodliness, the Lord put them a question. 'If then I be a father, where is mine honour? and if I be a master, where is my fear?' (Malachi 1:6). He was not given that honour and fear which was his due as Master in his own house. Although they professed to call him Father and Master, they had

174

departed from his ordinances. They were holding back what was due to him. They were robbing the Lord of his worship, of tithes and offerings, and not giving him that honour which was his due by seeking to uphold and advance his cause. But his people seek to honour him as their Lord and Master.

The word 'master' also means 'schoolmaster'. He teaches them by his Word and Spirit, and brings them into his own school. The word 'disciple' means 'pupil', and they are all taught by him, from the least unto the greatest. He teaches them through the dispensations of his providence so that none need say to his brother, 'Know the LORD.' They seek to sit at his feet and learn of him.

That has reference to the inward teaching of the Holy Spirit. Christ by his Word and Spirit teaches his people inwardly, and he also teaches them by his dealings with them in providence, in which they are brought to see the hand of the Lord and to submit to him.

This does not rule out the ministry of the Word. The Lord also teaches through the outward ministry. As the apostle points out in the epistle to the Ephesians, the ministry is given to the saints for the edifying of the body of Christ—that is, his mystical body—that they might be built up in their most holy faith. Through the outward ministry they are fed and taught, the Lord blessing it to their souls.

They are given that spiritual knowledge which the Lord alone can give. When he gives that knowledge, his people are brought to reverence and follow him. They seek to honour him. As he said to the disciples, 'Ye call me Master and Lord. ... If ye know these things, happy are ye if

ONE THING IS NEEDFUL

ye do them.' (John 13:13, 17). That is, if they would follow his example. For he left them an example that they should follow in his footsteps, and that is one of the ways in which they can honour him as their Lord and Master. In this particular instance in John 13 he washed their feet. 'If I then, your Lord and Master, have washed your feet; ye also ought to wash one another's feet.' He was willing to receive them and to forgive them their sins in washing their feet, for they sin daily—they go astray—and they need daily to be cleansed. He is rich in mercy and will be washing their feet as long as they are in this world, carrying on the work of sanctification in their souls.

When he is so ready to forgive, they should seek to exercise the same spirit of charity and forgiveness towards the brethren when they offend or sin against them. Oh, that they would seek to wash their feet and cherish a spirit of forgiveness, and not a spirit of revenge or a vindictive spirit, toward them! Oh, that they would leave all matters in the hand of him who said, 'Vengeance is mine; I will repay, saith the Lord' (Romans 12:19). It is better to commit our ways to the Lord and not to take matters into our own hands. I heard of a man who once said, 'I'll have my revenge,' and his brother said to him, 'If you'll have your revenge you'll be stealing it, for "Vengeance is mine; I will repay, saith the Lord."' His people seek to acknowledge him as their Lord and Master.

3. Implications of the message

Now we have in the last place a few things implied in the message: 'The Master is come, and calleth for thee.'

The message was to Mary in her disconsolate condition. She was at home weeping over the loss she had sustained through the death of her brother Lazarus. But as soon as she heard these words, she arose quickly and came to Jesus. There was in this message a call to Mary to see the compassion of the Lord.

Later she would go forth to the grave where Jesus was. There Jesus wept. She perceived in Jesus' tears a proof of his compassion. No doubt when her faith was tried—when Christ delayed for two days—unbelief and Satan put their own construction on the delay. And when Lazarus got worse and at last died and was buried in the grave, everything seemed to point to the fact that Christ did not have compassion. She may have been using the words of the Psalmist: 'Forever will the Lord cast off, / and gracious be no more? / Forever is his mercy gone? / Fails his word evermore? / Is't true that to be gracious / the Lord forgotten hath? /And that his tender mercies he / hath shut up in his wrath?' (Psalm 77:7–9). Matters in providence would indicate that it was so. But now she was given a revelation of the compassion of the Saviour and a proof thereof in his tears. 'His compassions fail not.' 'In all their afflictions,' we read, 'he was afflicted.' He has a fellow feeling with his people in their afflictions and trials. 'For we have not an high priest which cannot be touched with the feeling of our infirmities; but was in all points tempted like as we are, yet without sin' (Hebrews 4:15).

Although he delayed, it is in connection with his abiding two days in the place where he was that we read that 'Jesus loved Martha, and her sister, and Lazarus'. Unbelief would say that there was want of love—want of compassion and want of fellow feeling in his delay. But this message opens up the compassion of the Saviour to Mary. She had to pass through all this trial in order to get proof that 'his compassions fail not'. Even when he delays and all is dark in providence; when his people are tried and tempted and even conclude as the disciples did, 'Carest thou not that we perish?' yet his compassions fail not. He has a fellow feeling with them in their infirmities and trials, and in his own time he will make that known to them as surely as he did to Mary when she saw his tears. 'Jesus wept.'

Then there was in the message, a call to see the Lord fulfilling his own promise. His time had come. It must be *his* time. We already remarked that Abraham had to wait twenty-five years for the fulfilment of the promise. He and Sarah took matters into their own hands—Sarah suggesting that he take Hagar the Egyptian handmaid to wife, and that he would have a son by Hagar. That way the promise would be fulfilled, they thought. There was Abraham, the father of the faithful, and Sarah, a godly woman, building upon the foundation hay, wood and stubble. They thought it would stand, that the Lord would accept of it. But instead, they went through many a fiery trial for trying to fulfil the promise in their own way and in their own time. The Lord burnt that up. He would not accept of Ishmael as the promised son.

How often it is true of the Lord's people that they are left to build and do things that are but hay, wood and stubble in God's sight, however right it may be in their own eyes. In love to their souls and in love to his own cause and to the foundation that he laid in Zion, the Lord burns that up. Though Abraham and Sarah waited twenty-five years, the Lord was going to fulfil his promise—just as later he would fulfil his promises to Joseph—when *his* time had come.

The Lord's time had now come to fulfil his promise to Martha and Mary, and the message 'The Master is come, and calleth for thee' was a call to see its fulfilment. It was 'through fire and water' that she came to this 'wealthy place'. It is true usually in the experience and history of his people that they go through trials before they are brought to a wealthy place, as the Psalmist says: 'Thou hast caus'd men ride o'er our heads; / and though that we did pass / through fire and water, yet thou brought'st / us to a wealthy place' (Psalm 66:12).

Jesus would also give them a manifestation of his power, as he said to Martha, 'Said I not unto thee, that, if thou wouldest believe, thou shouldest see the glory of God?' He manifested forth his glory and his power in calling Lazarus from the dead. See how unbelief was uppermost in the case of Martha when Christ told them to remove the stone. She said, 'Lord, by this time he stinketh: for he hath been dead four days.'

Jesus cried with a loud voice, 'Lazarus, come forth. And he that was dead came forth, bound hand and foot with graveclothes: and his face was bound about with a napkin. Jesus saith unto them, Loose him, and let him go.' Somebody has remarked that if Christ had simply said, 'Come forth,' all in the graves would have come forth. There was power in his voice—it was the voice of the Son of God. He created all things by the word of his power; by the word of his power he raised Lazarus from the dead.

Here he gave a revelation of himself as the resurrection and the life. He is the resurrection and the life in a spiritu-

179

al sense in calling sinners out of the grave of a state of nature. As he says, 'The hour is coming, and now is, when
the dead shall hear the voice of the Son of God: and they
that hear shall live' (John 5:25). His voice in the gospel
draws the soul to himself. He quickens 'the soul in sin that
lies'. Lazarus was bound hand and foot, and his face was
bound about with a napkin. So the soul that is brought to
the Saviour is bound, as it were—he takes matters of the
grave with him. There is much spiritual deadness and
blindness. But although Lazarus was bound like that, there
was life in his soul. You don't expect the person who is
newly born to have the knowledge of a father—to attain
to the attainments of others. There are just babes in grace
who need much instruction and nursing, and there is
much that needs to be removed. That is part of the duty
of the church, to be loosening what encumbers the new-
born babes and what will be a weight to them, by pointing out the things they should give up and by instructing
them.

Life will prove itself. If the Lord has quickened a soul,
however blind that poor sinner may be to begin with, and
however burdened with many encumbrances, as he goes
on in his wilderness journey he will see his need of getting
rid of those things, and the Lord will give him instructors.
The Good Samaritan came to the succour of the man
who fell among thieves, and 'went to him and bound up
his wounds, pouring in oil and wine, and set him on his
own beast, and brought him to an inn' and said to the
innkeeper, 'Take care of him.' He put him in the care of
the innkeeper. So the Lord in his mercy deals with any
poor sinner he brings in. He puts that sinner in the care of
some person and in the care of the church.

You don't expect a baby to grow into a man or a woman all at once. There's something far wrong with a person who was never a child but was almost full-grown when born. There's something unnatural about that. The late Mr Macfarlane, Dingwall, heard a divinity student preaching for the first time. When asked what he thought of this young man who had a growing reputation, Mr Macfarlane said, 'Too old, too old.' He appeared to be too old for his years. And so indeed it proved to be.

To begin with, the sinner called by Christ needs instruction. He needs light, but if there is the light of grace in his soul, he will be growing in grace and in the knowledge of our Lord and Saviour Jesus Christ. Christ is the resurrection of his people—he resurrected them out of a state of nature—and he is their life. They have a life of faith upon him, 'for the just shall live by faith'.

As surely as he called Lazarus out of the grave, Christ shall call the dead out of their graves at the last day. 'Marvel not at this: for the hour is coming, in the which all that are in the graves shall hear his voice, and shall come forth; they that have done good unto the resurrection of life; and they that have done evil, unto the resurrection of damnation' (John 5:28–29).

We see here a reunion between Lazarus and his sisters, and it is true that at the last day there will be a reunion of his people. They shall be together as to their souls in glory. We are told that they are 'come ... to the spirits of just men made perfect' (Hebrews 12:23). That implies knowledge. Their coming to them implies fellowship with them. On the morning of the resurrection they shall be 'forever with the Lord'. Those who die in the Lord shall be together with the Lord. The apostle makes that clear in his first epistle to the Thessalonians: those who were sorrowing for their friends were to 'comfort one another with these words' (1 Thessalonians 4:18). They fully believed they had died in the Lord, but they missed their fellowship and company. That is legitimate sorrow— the Lord himself sorrowed at the grave of Lazarus. They were not sorrowing 'even as others which have no hope' (1 Thessalonians 4:13), but they were comforted that their friends who had died were with the Lord. As Jonathan Edwards points out, though they were now mourning the loss of the companionship and fellowship they had had with them, that fellowship and communion would be restored in heaven.

Christ comes in the free call of the gospel as the resurrection and the life. He says to sinners, 'The Master is come, and calleth for thee.' It is a personal call. When Christ is thus set before us in the gospel, we should be praying that he would give us a resurrection in our own souls' experience and that we would be found among the living in Jerusalem, that Christ would be our life, that we would be enabled to say with the Psalmist, 'The LORD is my light and my salvation … the LORD is the strength of my life' (Psalm 27:1).

He is the life of his own and they seek to live a life of faith upon him. He says, 'Because I live, ye shall live also.' They may at times feel as if their spiritual life is extinguished, and that grace has just died in their souls. But he will revive them. 'My soul he doth restore again; / and me to walk doth make / within the paths of righteousness, / ev'n for his own name's sake' (Psalm 23:3).

He will restore the souls of his own according to his promise: 'Because I live, ye shall live also.' He is alive after the power of an endless life, making continual intercession for them. He will revive them according to the promise: 'When the poor and needy seek water, and there is none, and their tongue faileth for thirst, I the LORD will hear them, I the God of Israel will not forsake them' (Isaiah 41:17).

'The Master is come and calleth for thee.' When Mary heard the message, she arose quickly and went to where the Saviour was. We should be going forth unto him, going forth 'without the camp, bearing his reproach' (Hebrews 15:15) and asking to have him as our life. These words, 'The Master is come, and calleth for thee', contain the message of the gospel. How we should be exercised over these words!

He calls his people effectually out of the grave of a state of nature, he shall call them at death to be forever with himself, and he shall call their bodies out of their graves at the resurrection. 'Gather my saints together unto me; those that have made a covenant with me by sacrifice' (Psalm 50:5). Their vile bodies he shall change and make like unto his glorious body, according to the power 'wherewith he is able to subdue all things unto himself'. They shall be forever with himself.

The Master *is* come. He has finished the work given him to do, and now in virtue of that work he is set before us in the gospel as the resurrection and the life, as the one in whom there is eternal life for lost and perishing sinners. For 'this is the record, that God has given to us eternal life, and this life is in his Son' (1 John 5:11). This is the sum and substance of the everlasting gospel. The Lord has given us eternal life in the free offer of the gospel, and we have that in the words of our text. 'The Master is come, and calleth for thee.'

May he bless his Truth.

The second coming

*For the Lord himself shall descend from heaven
with a shout, with the voice of the archangel,
and with the trump of God: and the dead in
Christ shall rise first: then we which are alive and
remain shall be caught up together with them in
the clouds, to meet the Lord in the air: and so
shall we ever be with the Lord.*

1 THESSALONIANS 4:16–17

IN these words we have the doctrine of the second
coming of the Lord Jesus Christ brought before us,
including what shall take place concerning his people
at his second coming. In many other parts of Scripture,
we are told what will take place in connection with those
who are not his people—what shall befall the wicked. But
the apostle here speaks of those who slept in Jesus and
who died in the Lord. 'Blessed are the dead which die in
the Lord' (Revelation14:13). He describes what shall take
place at the resurrection when Christ comes the second
time, both in connection with those who died in Jesus,
and also what shall take place regarding the Lord's people
who are alive on that day.

1. We may therefore, as enabled, make a few remarks in the first place on the second coming of the Lord.

2. In the second place, we may make some remarks on what we are told shall take place concerning his people. We are told that first of all the dead in Christ shall rise first: that is, those who were in Christ in this world and have died before his second coming. Then we are told what shall befall those of his people who are alive when he comes (verse 17).

1. The second coming of Christ

In the first place, a few remarks about the second coming of Christ. When we speak about his second coming, that implies that there was a first coming—his first advent. We have here his second advent. These two comings, or advents, are clearly brought before us by the apostle in his epistle to the Hebrews: 'And as it is appointed unto men once to die, but after this the judgment: so Christ was once offered to bear the sins of many; and unto them that look for him shall he appear the second time without sin unto salvation' (Hebrews 9:27–28).

He appeared the first time in the flesh when he was born in Bethlehem. He appeared in human nature—he took to himself human nature in the womb of the virgin. He appeared to this end: to bear the sins of many. 'But now once in the end of the world hath he appeared to put away sin by the sacrifice of himself' (Hebrews 9:26). 'The end of the world' there means the end of the Old Testament dispensation. Christ's death put an end to that world. As this epistle mentions, the Lord shook their heavens and their earth—that is, their religious and political world. That was the end of their world.

'Christ was once offered to bear the sins of many.' We have there in brief compass the purpose of his first advent, his first coming into the world—to bear the sins of many, to put away the sin of his people by the sacrifice of himself. And he is to appear a second time on the day of judgment. We are told that after death is the judgment: this has reference to the great day of judgment. Though men are judged at death, they shall be openly judged at the great day of judgment. Christ will then appear 'the second time without sin'. The first time he appeared he was bearing the sins of many: he was the sin bearer. But now the second time he shall not come as a man of sorrows and acquainted with grief, to offer himself a sacrifice. He did that in the days of his flesh. He shall appear the second time unto salvation unto them that look for him. He will appear as the Saviour of his people: 'Unto them that look for him shall he appear the second time without sin unto salvation.'

It is then that their bodies shall be raised and made like unto Christ's glorious body, and they shall enter then into the fulness of the salvation which he procured for them. At death their souls enter into the joy of the Lord, for their souls are made perfect in holiness at death. 'But their bodies, being still united to Christ, do rest in their graves till the resurrection.' It is at the second coming of Christ that their salvation shall be complete, that their bodies shall be raised and made like unto his glorious body.

We have there brought before us in brief compass the two advents of the Lord: his first, to bear the sins of many, and to offer himself a sacrifice to satisfy divine justice and to reconcile us to God; and the second time, at the judgment, he will appear without sin unto salvation to them who look for him, that is, to his people who are looking to him and believing on him. There are many proofs given in the Word of God of the second coming of Christ and of the resurrection. On his coming the dead shall be raised. There shall be a resurrection of the just and of the unjust. In 1 Corinthians 15 the apostle through the Holy Spirit proves the doctrine of the second coming of Christ, the day of judgment, and the resurrection, in the light of Christ's own resurrection. The great proof we have that the dead shall rise at the last day is Christ's own resurrection from the dead. It is the great proof that we have that he shall come at the last day, 'in righteousness to judge the world, / justice to give each one' (Psalm 9:8).

In 1 Corinthians 15, Christ is spoken of as the firstfruits of them that slept. 'For since by man came death, by man came also the resurrection of the dead' (verse 21). By the first Adam came death through his sin; by the second Adam, the Lord from heaven, came the resurrection from the dead. 'How', asks the apostle, 'is Christ risen from the dead, and become the firstfruits of them that slept?' (verse 20). The firstfruits of the harvest was a pledge that the whole harvest would be gathered in. Christ entered heaven as the pledge and proof that the whole harvest of the election of grace shall be gathered into the heavenly garner.

Among the feasts of the Old Testament church there was the feast of the firstfruits. When the harvest was ripe, a sheaf of the firstfruits was cut and presented in the temple before the Lord. That feast was held, as the Word of God tells us, on the day after the Sabbath. Mention of the firstfruits reminds me of a thought about Christ, spoken of as the firstfruits in connection with his resurrection. Whereas the feast of the passover pointed to the death of Christ, the feast of the firstfruits pointed to his resurrection from the dead. It took place on the day after the Sabbath, that is, on the first day of the week, the day on which the Saviour rose from the grave. We have there another evidence that the day on which the Saviour rose was to be the day that would commemorate his resurrection. The Lord's Day now commemorates Christ's resurrection from the dead. Every Sabbath therefore reminds us that Christ rose from the dead.

The Sabbath also reminds us of Christ's second coming, for his resurrection is the guarantee that we have of his second coming, and of the resurrection of the dead. This is clearly brought before us in the verse that says: 'God … now commandeth all men everywhere to repent: because he hath appointed a day, in the which he will judge the world in righteousness by that man whom he hath ordained; whereof he hath given assurance unto all men, in that he hath raised him from the dead' (Acts 17:30–31). The assurance God has given of the day of judgment is that he has raised Christ from the dead. That is the assurance that the great day of judgment will take place. In view of that day, the day of death will be to each of us a day of judgment, for then we shall be judged.

Those who are in Christ shall not come into condemnation, either at death or at the judgment, but all who die without repentance shall be condemned at death and openly condemned at the great day of judgment. In view of these solemn realities God now commands all men—*all*

189

men—everywhere to repent. It is God who is calling upon you to repent. It is God who is commanding you to
repent. It is no apostle or angel or minister who is calling
upon you to repent, but God, the judge of all, commands
all men everywhere to repent. As Christ himself says, 'Except ye repent, ye shall all likewise perish' (Luke 13:3).

We are told here, in connection with his coming at the
last day to raise the dead and to judge the living and the
dead, that 'the Lord himself shall descend from heaven
with a shout'. He is to come in person. He came on the
day of Pentecost in the power of the Holy Spirit, and he
has come many a time since—at times of revival—in the
power of the Holy Spirit. He comes in the case of every
sinner who is born again: he comes to that sinner in his
Word and Spirit. It is through his Word and Spirit that he
dwells in the souls of his people. He not only comes in
mercy in the power of the Holy Spirit in connection with
his Word and gospel, but he has often come in judgment.
He has not yet come personally, but it is the Lord who
comes forth out of his place when judgments occur. We
speak of the judgments of the Lord, and it is the Lord
coming forth—not in person, but making use of instru-
ments for the execution of his judgments.

We have proof of that in Matthew chapter 16, where
Christ says, 'For the Son of man shall come in the glory of
his Father with his angels; and then he shall reward every
man according to his works' (verse 27). This refers to the
great day. But then he says in the next verse, 'Verily I say
unto you, There be some standing here, which shall not
taste of death, till they see the Son of man coming in his
kingdom.' Christ came in his kingdom at Pentecost
through the power of the Holy Spirit, when the New

Testament dispensation of the kingdom was established. In verse 27 he speaks of his personal coming at the last day; in verse 28 he speaks of his coming in the power of the Holy Spirit—on the day of Pentecost, in times of revival, and as he does in the case of every sinner who is called effectually.

But now we read here that at the last day the Lord himself shall descend. He is to come in person at his second coming, when he comes without sin unto salvation to them that look for him. He himself shall descend from heaven with a shout, 'with the voice of the archangel' and so on. We read that the angels shall come with him, and there may be an archangel leading the heavenly hosts. There are ten thousand times ten thousand, and thousands of thousands of angels. They shall accompany him when he comes in the glory of his Father to sit upon the great white throne, to judge the world in righteousness.

It is at the sound of the last trump that the dead shall be raised. And by that we are to understand Christ himself: the voice of his human nature—the power of his Godhead manifest through his human nature. At the grave of Lazarus he had but to say, 'Lazarus, come forth,' and he that was dead came forth. It was the same voice that created all things by the word of his power. He called the worlds out of the womb of nothingness by the word of his power. On the great day he has but to speak the word and all who are in their graves shall come forth. In the Gospel of John we read, 'Marvel not at this: for the hour is coming, in the which all that are in the graves shall hear his voice, and shall come forth; they that have done good, unto the resurrection of life; and they that have done evil, unto the resurrection of damnation' (chapter 6:28–29).

191

There will be a resurrection of the just and of the unjust. And at his voice, which called Lazarus from the grave, every corpse shall forth out of its grave. We read that the sea shall give up her dead.

All shall be there before him: those who arise to the resurrection of life (his people), and those who have done evil to the resurrection of damnation. We have in his own words how he shall pronounce the sentence, how he shall put the sheep on his right hand and the wicked—the goats—on his left. He shall say to those on his right hand, 'Come, ye blessed of my Father, inherit the kingdom prepared for you from the foundation of the world.' And to those on his left he shall say, 'Depart from me, ye cursed, into everlasting fire, prepared for the devil and his angels.' And you and I shall be there. We know that every eye shall see Christ when he comes at his second advent, when he himself shall descend from heaven. He shall come in the clouds of heaven, and every eye shall see him—the righteous and the wicked. Every eye shall see the Judge, and you and I shall be there. We shall be either on the right hand or on the left.

We are still on mercy's ground, and in view of that solemn day, as already mentioned, 'God now commandeth all men everywhere to repent'. Those who did not repent shall be on the left; those who did repent shall be on the right hand. We are commanded to repent. Our responsibility is brought before us as rational, responsible creatures: 'Repent.' God the Father commands you to repent. God the Son commands you to repent. And God the Holy Ghost commands you to repent. 'Let the wicked forsake his way, and the unrighteous man his thoughts: and let him return unto the LORD, and he will have mercy

upon him; and to our God, for he will abundantly pardon' (Isaiah 55:7).

2. The Lord's people at the day of judgment

We shall now notice, in the second place, what shall take
place in connection with the Lord's people at the great
day of judgment. That is what is brought before us here.

Paul speaks of those who slept in Jesus. 'Them also which
sleep in Jesus will God bring with him' (verse 14). We are
told here that when the trump of God shall sound and the
dead shall be raised, the dead in Christ shall rise first.

They died in Christ. 'Blessed are the dead which die in
the Lord' (Revelation 14:15). That shows that they were
alive in Christ in this world. There was a day in their history when they were not in Christ, when they were
without hope and without God in the world. But this
takes place in the case of all who shall die in the Lord—
who will have a blessed death and a blessed resurrection:
they come to be in Christ.

'Therefore if any man be in Christ, he is a new creature:
old things are passed away; behold, all things are become
new' (2 Corinthians 5:17). They had a spiritual resurrection in their souls' experience, as we read of the Ephesians: 'You hath he quickened who were dead in trespasses and sins' (Ephesians 2:1). In John chapter 5 Christ says,
'The hour is coming, and now is, when the dead shall
hear the voice of the son of God: and they that hear shall
live.' That is, they hear his voice in the gospel. They hear
his voice in the law, condemning them because of their
sin, and they hear his voice in the gospel, bringing peace
into their souls. They become the sheep of his pasture.

They are found repenting through hearing his voice. It is Christ's voice—the Word of God—that is calling upon us to repent. Those who hear his voice are repentant sinners. They repent of their sins and turn to the Lord. They hear his voice in the law and they hear his voice in the gospel. 'My sheep hear my voice, and I know them, and they follow me; and I give unto them eternal life; and they shall never perish, neither shall any man pluck them out of my hand' (John 10:27–28).

'Blessed and holy is he that hath part in the first resurrection: on such the second death hath no power' (Revelation 20:6). The two resurrections are described in John chapter 5. First, the spiritual resurrection: the soul is quickened through hearing the voice of Christ, and the soul proves that he has been quickened by now following Christ in the world, following the Good Shepherd through good and evil report. That is a spiritual resurrection: it is the first resurrection. The second resurrection will be at the great day. Those who are thus spiritually quickened in their souls, who have this resurrection in their souls, are said to be blessed. 'O greatly bless'd the people are / the joyful sound that know; / in brightness of thy face, O Lord, / they ever on shall go' (Psalm 89:15). They are also said to be holy, and they are being sanctified through the Truth. 'On such the second death hath no power' (Revelation 20:6).

The first and second resurrections

Premillenarians hold that by the first resurrection mentioned in Revelation 20:6 we are to understand a literal resurrection. They hold that Christ is to come at the beginning of the millennium, and that the saints and martyrs shall be raised at the beginning of the millennium, and that Christ will reign in the world for a thousand years. Then, they say, at the end of that thousand years shall be the day of judgment. That is why they are called premillenarians: 'pre-' means 'before'.

Those who hold that Christ will come in the power and demonstration of the Holy Spirit at the millennium, and that his second coming is at the day of judgment when he shall come to raise the dead and to judge the dead, are called Postmillenarians. 'Post-' means 'after'. It is after the millennium, and after the apostasy at the end of the millennium, that Christ will come.

Premillenarians therefore hold that the 'first resurrection' in Revelation 20:5–6 is to be understood literally—that the saints are to rise and to reign in this world with Christ for a thousand years. We hold that the first resurrection is on the contrary a spiritual resurrection, such as took place on the day of Pentecost when thousands were quickened in their souls and made new creatures in Christ Jesus. The Jews are to be gathered in, not in heaven, but in this world. They are to be grafted into their own stock—into the church. We are told that their ingathering shall be as life from the dead. That will be in connection with the fulness of the Gentiles. 'Fulness' in the Greek means 'multitude'. Multitudes of the Gentiles shall be converted, and the Jews shall be gathered in. That will be a resurrection: their conversion to Christ is spoken of as a resurrection from the dead. They are now dead spiritually, but God will work the resurrection of a nation.

Doubtless the millennium will be a worldwide resurrection, when multitudes of Gentiles from all lands, and the Jews, shall be gathered in through the outpouring of the

Holy Spirit. That will be just like a resurrection taking place—in China and Japan and America and in all lands of the earth. It will be a spiritual resurrection; there will not be a literal resurrection. We cannot accept the latter in the light of what Christ himself says: 'This is the Father's will which hath sent me, that of all which he hath given me I should lose nothing, but should raise it up again at the last day' (John 6:39). This is one of the most convincing arguments that show that by the first resurrection in Revelation chapter 20 we are to understand not a literal resurrection but a spiritual resurrection. The whole election of grace is to be literally raised up at the last day.

Christ continues: 'And this is the will of him that sent me, that every one which seeth the Son, and believeth on him, may have everlasting life: and I will raise him up at the last day.' He says also, 'No man can come to me, except the Father which hath sent me draw him: and I will raise him up at the last day.' And, 'Whoso eateth my flesh, and drinketh my blood hath eternal life; and I will raise him up at the last day' (John 6:40, 44, 54).

Why all the emphasis on raising him up at the last day? All that the Father gave to Christ—the whole election of grace—he will raise up at the last day. Everyone who believes in Christ, who is taught of the Father, Christ shall raise up at the last day. Those who live a life of faith upon Christ—who eat his flesh and drink his blood—he shall raise up at the last day. That shows it is at the last day that persons are to be resurrected. And Christ emphasises this, as if he were forestalling all these interpretations. From what he says here in John 6, we can only conclude that the first resurrection spoken of in Revelation chapter 20 is a spiritual resurrection—a resurrection of souls, not of bodies. Just as Elijah had a resurrection in John the Baptist, so shall martyrs have a resurrection yet. Luthers shall arise in Germany, and Calvins in France; Knoxes shall arise in Scotland, and divines like Voetius[5] and Mastricht[6] in Holland, and in other parts. They shall arise and defend these doctrines.

One of the most conclusive proofs that we have that that resurrection described in Revelation chapter 20 is a spiritual resurrection is that Christ says time and time again that it is not until the last day that he will raise his people. And those passages in John make clear that it is at the last day that they will all come out of their graves, some to the resurrection of life and some to the resurrection of damnation.

It is true of all his people that they have a spiritual resurrection. They are a blessed people, whose God is the Lord. They prove that they have had a spiritual resurrection by seeking to follow holiness, 'without which no man shall see the Lord'. Over such, the second death shall have no power. As Christ says, 'He that heareth my word, and believeth on him that sent me, hath everlasting life, and shall not come into condemnation; but is passed from death unto life' (John 5:24). In other words, he shall not be hurt by the second death.

---

[5] Gisbertus Voetius in the Latinized form of the Dutch name Gijsbert Voet (1589–1677), who was an eminent Professor of Theology at Utrecht from 1634.
[6] Petrus (or Peter) van Mastricht (1630–1706) was successor to Voetius at Utrecht, and was likewise highly esteemed for his theological writings.

The dead in Christ

'The dead in Christ' are persons who died in Christ, and who were in Christ. They had a spiritual resurrection, and death did not separate them from Christ. As the apostle says in Romans, neither distresses nor tribulations, nor principalities nor powers, nor anything can separate his people from his love. And death will not separate his people from Christ. They sleep in Christ. That is why the death of the Lord's people is spoken of as a sleep. They sleep in Christ. They have been in Christ, and 'them also which sleep in Jesus will God bring with him'.

Death cannot separate them from Christ, and no distress or tribulation can separate them from Christ. The great Dr Hugh Martin[7] used to be mentally ill at times. His affliction caused him sometimes to be confined. He used to say, 'Should I die insane, I shall die in Christ.' Insanity would not separate his soul from Christ, or rob him of his interest in Christ. No distress or tribulation—no imbalance of the mind or dissolution of the body—can separate his people from Christ. They sleep in the Saviour, and them who sleep in Jesus God will bring with him.

It is also mentioned that 'we which are alive and remain unto the coming of the Lord shall not prevent them which are asleep'. Here 'prevent' is an old English word which means 'to go before'. Although we might be alive when Christ comes, we shall not have the better of them that sleep. We are told here in the Word of the Lord that

---

[7] Hugh Martin (1822–1885) was the Free Church minister of Panbride near Carnoustie, Angus, from 1844 until 1858 when he was translated to the Free Greyfriars congregation in Edinburgh. Poor health forced him to take early retirement from the ministry in 1865.

'the dead in Christ shall rise first', and then we who are alive shall be changed. The apostle mentions this in 1 Corinthians: 'Behold, I shew you a mystery; we shall not all sleep, but we shall all be changed, in a moment, in the twinkling of an eye, at the last trump: for the trumpet shall sound, and the dead shall be raised incorruptible, and we shall be changed' (chapter 15:51–52). Those who are alive shall neither sleep nor die, but shall be changed in a moment. Their mortal bodies shall be changed when the last trumpet sounds at the second coming of Christ at the last day.

Premillenarians believe that all this will take place at the beginning of the millennium; that those who are alive shall be changed in the twinkling of an eye and caught up in the clouds to meet the Lord in the air, along with those who have been resurrected. They call that 'the rapture'. The word 'rapture' means 'to be caught up'. Some premillenarians hold that after the rapture the church of God will go through 'the tribulation'. We read in Revelation of those who were before the throne clothed in white robes, whom John was told had come out of 'great tribulation'. Premillenarians maintain there is to be a period of great tribulation for seven years; the seventieth week in Daniel, they say, is to be a period of great tribulation. Some of them hold that the church of God will suffer the tribulation: some that the rapture will take place before the tribulation. And those who follow Scofield's Bible (who are called dispensationalists) hold that the Lord's people are to be raptured before the tribulation.

Of course the Lord's people are often in tribulation of a different sort. Christ himself said, 'In the world ye shall have tribulation' (John 16:33). And it is through much tribulation that they shall enter into the kingdom of heaven. But dispensationalists are expecting a special tribulation.

Not all premillenarians are dispensationalists. Dispensationalists divide the Bible into so many dispensations. When I was preparing this sermon, I thought I would refresh my memory as to their beliefs. I was astounded when I began to study the views that the dispensationalists hold in connection with the resurrection. We ought to be acquainted with those things. There are many schools of premillenarians. Some hold that the church is to go through what they call the tribulation. But, on the other hand, dispensationalists hold that the rapture occurs before the tribulation, and that the church therefore does not go through the tribulation; that Christ's coming is without further signs and may occur at any moment; and that, following the rapture, Christ and his people are to be in the air for a period of seven years (that is, the seventieth week of Daniel's prophecy, according to their interpretation). During these seven years, they believe, there shall be great tribulation in this world. Then the Antichrist is to appear.

One of the leading dispensationalists, DeHaan, describes the rapture in this way: 'One of these days, as sure as this is the Word of God, those who have pled with you, who have warned you, who have prayed for you, will be missing. … In a moment the streets are full of people, weeping, crying and howling over the disappearance of loved ones. What has happened? The Lord has come, like a thief in the night. He has quietly stolen away those who trusted him, like Enoch, and no one is left behind to warn you any more, to pray or show you the way.'[8]

I shall also quote a book by Dr Bishop's, which he calls *The Doctrines of Grace*.[9] 'When Christ comes the invisible church will be caught up out of the midst of the visible. It will be a secret rapture. ... Only a few here and there will wake up and say, "It is too late! I am left out. My godly relations have gone—the Spirit of God has departed. The reign of evil unchecked has begun. Foolish Virgins—Foolish Virgins! We have slept away our day of grace. It is too late!"'

They also say that at the end of the seven-year rapture, they are to come back to this world (at the end of the tribulation). It is then that Christ is to set up his kingdom in this world, or so dispensationalists hold. But dispensationalism has this startling feature: they say that the Holy Spirit is to be taken out of the world when the church is raptured. Standard premillenarian doctrine has it that the Holy Spirit was given at Pentecost, at which time the church was especially equipped for his work of world evangelism. Throughout the rapture, with the departure of the church, the Holy Spirit is withdrawn from the world. The Scofield Bible expresses it thus: 'After the Holy Spirit is taken out of the way.' Then begins the tribulation of seven years, and it is then that the Antichrist is said to appear. Dispensationalists do not believe that the Antichrist has already appeared. They discard the Reformation doctrine that the Papacy is the Antichrist.

---

[8] Rev. Richard W. DeHaan, Radio Bible Class, Grand Rapids, Michigan. November 1954.
[9] George Sayles Bishop, *The Doctrines of Grace* (New York: Gospel Publishing House, 1910).

Another remarkable theory of theirs is that during the tribulation the Jews are to be converted, but not through the Holy Spirit, for the Holy Spirit is taken away. According to dispensationalists, the Jews are to be converted through seeing Christ standing on the Mount of Olives when he comes for the church. The Jews, so this theory holds, are to be converted by the mere sight of Christ, the Messiah, on the Mount of Olives, and through their testimony all nations are to be converted. We must point out, however, that people were not converted at the mere sight of Jesus at the time of his first advent, and that it is the particular work of the Holy Spirit to regenerate the soul and give it new vision to enable it to turn to Christ. The mere presence of Christ often had the effect of hardening his enemies rather than converting them. Yet, according to dispensationalists, Christ standing on the Mount of Olives when he returns for his church signifies the conversion of the Jews without the Holy Spirit, and then the Jews are to start converting the Gentiles, also without the Holy Spirit.

This comment is made on their theory: 'How could they be regenerated if there were no Holy Spirit present to give them the new birth?' The whole theory is thoroughly unscriptural, since it would by inference deny that man is dead in sins, and thus contradict Ephesians chapters 1 and 2.

It has also been pointed out that in the supposed conversion of the Jews without the Holy Spirit, dispensationalism sets forth among other things the doctrine of a 'second chance'. If you are not converted by the Holy Spirit, you can be converted during the tribulation! The doctrine of a second opportunity of salvation in a later dispensation is held forth to these who are living at the time of the rapture.

That is what the dispensationalists believe. They maintain that, after the seven years, they will return and set up the 'millennial kingdom', and it is then that the gospel of the kingdom will be preached. They believe that large portions of the Sermon on the Mount, and all the parables, and other parts of the Bible, belong to the gospel of the kingdom and not to the 'Church Age'. So, according to them, we have nothing to do with the Sermon on the Mount and with large portions of the Scriptures. These passages supposedly apply to this other dispensation that will be ushered in at the end of the tribulation, when the 'millennial kingdom' shall be set up.

That is only part of the dispensational system. To deal with their theories on the Old Testament, on the Law, would take too long. But as regarding the Holy Spirit being withdrawn and sinners converted, etc., this whole theory can be condemned as unscriptural throughout. Yet because these theories are popularised and becoming fashionable, it is good to know more about them.

Resurrection and judgment

In conclusion, at the last day there will be the resurrection and the judgment. We find the apostles putting the question to Christ, 'Tell us, when shall these things be? and what shall be the sign of thy coming, and of the end of the world?' (Matthew 24:3). The word 'end' is translated from the Greek word *sunteleia* (συντέλεια) meaning a 'full end', according to Young's Analytical Concordance. This word is used only six times in the New Testament, and it always designates the judgment day—that is, the end of the world.

Before his ascension Jesus gave his disciples the well-known command, 'Go ye therefore, and teach all nations.' He concludes, 'Lo, I am with you alway, even unto the end of the world' (Matthew 28:19–20). The word *sun-teleia* is again used there: the 'full end'. Jesus would not have commanded his church to preach the gospel until the judgment day if a rapture preceded the event. The fact is that Jesus did not provide any channels for disseminating the gospel other than the church. When that task is done—when the gospel has been preached to all the world—then the end comes. But the church must be in the world to the full end of the age in order for Christ to be with us as long as he has promised.

Christ gives a detailed account of the sequence of events at the end of the age in Matthew chapter 13 in the parable of the tares. 'The enemy that sowed them is the devil; the harvest is the end (*sunteleia*—the *full* end) of the world; the reapers are the angels. As therefore the tares are gathered and burned in the fire; so shall it be in the end of this world' (Matthew 13:39–40). The angels shall come forth and sever the wicked from the just. The use of that Greek word in each of these verses absolutely precludes the possibility of the righteous being taken out of the world before the full end of the age. Both the righteous and the wicked grow together until the end of the world. Many of Christ's parables show that he is to come at the end of the world, and there will be a resurrection of the just and of the unjust.

The Lord declares that he will 'pour upon the house of David, and upon the inhabitants of Jerusalem, the spirit of grace and of supplications: and they shall look upon me whom they have pierced, and they shall mourn for him, as one mourneth for his only son' (Zechariah 12:10).

False views are widespread in our day, and people preach them as if they were the Word of God and not merely their own thoughts and interpretations. The law of God is set aside.

But these solemn matters are brought before us: 'The Lord himself shall descend from heaven with a shout, with the voice of the archangel, and with the trump of God: and the dead in Christ shall rise first: then we which are alive and remain shall be caught up together with them in the clouds to meet the Lord in the air: and go shall we ever be with the Lord.' We ought to be seeking preparation for death and for eternity, seeking to be of those who shall sleep in Jesus. 'Them also which sleep in Jesus will God bring with him.'

May he bless his Truth.

.

The lively hope

Blessed be the God and Father of our Lord Jesus Christ, which according to his abundant mercy hath begotten us again unto a lively hope by the resurrection of Jesus Christ from the dead, to an inheritance incorruptible, and undefiled, and that fadeth not away, reserved in heaven for you.

1 PETER 1:3–4

PETER is writing to 'the strangers scattered throughout Pontus, Galatia, Cappadocia, Asia, and Bithynia'. He describes them as being 'elect according to the foreknowledge of God the Father, through sanctification of the Spirit, unto obedience and sprinkling of the blood of Jesus Christ'. They were elected to obtain these blessings according to the foreknowledge of the Father: that is, the knowledge he took of them in a past eternity in making choice of them according to the good pleasure of his will. Foreknowledge means fore-love: he loved them with an everlasting love. 'For whom he did foreknow, he also did predestinate to be conformed to the image of his Son. … Whom he did predestinate, them he also called: and whom he called, them he also justified:

and whom he justified, them he also glorified' (Romans 8:29–30).

They were elected to receive these blessings, to be made partakers of the redemption purchased by Christ. They are made partakers of these blessings 'through sanctification of the Spirit'—that is, through the gracious teaching of God's Holy Spirit. They are washed with the washing of regeneration and called to good works—to walk in obedience. They have the spirit of adoption and they show this by seeking to give obedience to the Truth. They are 'born again, not of corruptible seed, but of incorruptible, by the word of God, which liveth and abideth for ever' (1 Peter 1:23). Where this is so, there will be the fruit of 'unfeigned love of the brethren' (1 Peter 1:22).

These are the persons who are here mentioned as having a 'lively hope'—having a good hope through grace—those who through the gracious teaching of the Spirit have been brought to a saving knowledge of the Saviour. They have been sprinkled with the blood, and show by their walk and conversation that they are giving obedience to Christ—the obedience of faith. In our text the apostle praises God for this blessing.

1. We may in the first place make a few remarks about those who have this 'lively hope'.

2. In the second place, the nature of the hope they have. It is said to be a 'lively hope' or a living hope.

3. And in the third place, we shall notice the blessings which are bound up with this hope. Embraced in this hope is an interest in the 'inheritance incorruptible, and undefiled, and that fadeth not away, reserved in heaven

for you' (verse 4). Those who have this lively hope are heirs of heaven, 'heirs of God, and joint heirs with Christ' (Romans 8:17).

1. The people who have a lively hope

In the first place, then, a few remarks on those who have this hope—this lively hope.

There was a day when they did not have this hope. They were without God and without hope in the world. That is true of all by nature. There are multitudes whose hopes are centred on worldly gain and worldly pleasures. The solemn realities of death, judgment and eternity, and their need of having this lively hope, do not enter their minds. They are engrossed in the things of this world, pursuing its gains and pleasures. Their hopes and their prospects are carnal and worldly: they are of the earth, earthy.

But we read of their end in Psalm 49: 'For he shall carry nothing hence, / when death his days doth end; / nor shall his glory after him / into the grave descend. / Although he his own soul did bless / whilst he on earth did live; / (and when thou to thyself dost well, / men will thee praises give;) / he to his fathers' race shall go, / they never shall see light. / Man honour'd wanting knowledge is / like beasts that perish quite' (verses 17–20). There you have the end of the worldling, who has his portion in this life only, who has no hope in view of death and of eternity, and who is not concerned as to whether he has a hope or not. As long as his worldly hopes and prospects prosper, that is all he is concerned about. But he will leave it all behind, and at death he will *not* enter into an inheritance 'incorruptible, and undefiled, and that fadeth not away'. His soul goes to a lost eternity.

And then there are multitudes more who profess to have a hope, and they never question the genuineness of their hope. They are religious after a manner, and well acquainted with the Scriptures, and they show a zeal for religion. They speak of what they give to God and what they do for God. That is what their hope is based on. If it is enquired what the foundation of their hope is, it will be found that it is not the fruit of their being made partakers of the redemption purchased by Christ. It is not a lively hope that they have, but the hope of the hypocrite which shall perish. The word 'hypocrite' at times in Scripture means a person who is self-deceived, as the foolish virgins were. They had the lamp of a hope and they fully expected that they would enter into the possession of this inheritance at death. But when death came, the lamp of their hope went out and they met with a shut door. And they were shut out for all eternity.

But in the case of those who have a good hope through grace, as we shall notice, it is not what they do or what they give, but what they hope that they receive from the Lord that is the foundation of their hope. 'Remember, Lord, thy gracious word / thou to thy servant spake, / which, for a ground of my sure hope, / thou causedst me to take' (Psalm 119:49).

This good hope is bound up with the resurrection of Jesus Christ from the dead. His resurrection from the dead implies his atoning death—an atonement for sinners that satisfied all the claims of God's law and justice. And as proof that God was well satisfied with the atonement which Christ made, he raised him from the dead. Not only that, but he exalted him to be a Prince and a Saviour, for to give repentance and remission of sins to Israel. In virtue of his resurrection from the dead—and all that is implied in that: his incarnation, his obedience unto death, the work that he finished—in virtue of that, he is set before us as a Prince and a Saviour, able to save to the uttermost. In virtue of the work that he accomplished, he is 'the hope of Israel, the saviour thereof in time of trouble' (Jeremiah 14:8). He is set before us as the *only* hope for lost and perishing sinners. Apart from him, there is no hope for us. How we should be cleaving to this hope! Those who have this good hope through grace have 'fled for refuge to lay hold upon the hope set before us' (Hebrews 6:18).

2. The lively hope

That leads us to consider in the second place the nature of their hope. Those who have Christ as their hope are said to have a lively hope—a living hope. That is because they have spiritual life. They were quickened. As we read, 'Ye are dead, and your life is hid with Christ in God' (Colossians 3:3). They came to die to every false hope that they had. They came to see that they had no hope in view of death and of eternity, that they were hopeless in themselves. It was in the day on which they were enabled to exercise faith in Christ that they came to have this good hope.

This living hope is not apart from faith in Christ. We read, 'Faith is the substance of things hoped for, the evidence of things not seen' (Hebrews 11:1). Faith sees a substance—a reality—in the blessings which are to be

211

found in Christ Jesus. And hope waits for these blessings; hope is the exercise of the soul toward Christ. The believer is led to wait with expectation for the blessings which are in Christ. As we read in Romans, 'We are saved by hope: but hope that is seen is not hope: for what a man seeth, why doth he yet hope for? But if we hope for that we see not, then do we with patience wait for it' (chapter 8:24–25).

They are saved by hope. That is, their hope is exercised in connection with the salvation that is in Christ Jesus. As Jacob on his deathbed confesses, 'I have waited for thy salvation, O LORD' (Genesis 49:18). Waiting is an exercise of hope: waiting with expectation, and looking to the Lord for the blessings which he is promising and offering in the everlasting gospel. Those who have faith see a reality in those blessings.

They are 'waiting for the adoption, to wit, the redemption of our body' (Romans 8:25). They expect that at death their souls will be made perfect in holiness, that the Lord will perfect that which concerneth them, that he will carry on the good work till the day of Jesus Christ. They are waiting for the fulness of salvation as far as their souls are concerned. They look to the Lord to sanctify them, and to prepare them for death and for eternity.

But also embraced in this lively hope are the 'groanings which cannot be uttered' (Romans 8:26)—groanings to be delivered from a body of sin and death, and to be sanctified and purified. These groanings and desires will be perfectly fulfilled as far as their souls are concerned at death, when their souls are made perfect in holiness, and as far as their bodies are concerned, on the morning of the resurrection, when they shall be made like unto Christ's glorious body.

These blessings are embraced in their hope, as the inheritance is. At death their souls are made perfect in holiness, and shall enter into the fulness of joy that is at God's right hand.

There is bound up in this hope a waiting upon the Lord, a looking to the Lord for the promised blessings. Those who have this hope are said to be a poor people, and it is their poverty that causes them to wait on the Lord. They go out to the means of grace in hope—the hope of getting what will sustain the life of their souls. It is a lively— a living—hope, and they need what will sustain their spiritual life. They go forth as Ruth went forth to glean in the fields of Boaz. They are therefore looking to the Lord for the supply of their needs. They hope in him, and 'the expectation of the poor / shall not be lost for aye' (Psalm 93:8).

Those who have the love of God shed abroad in their hearts are constrained to live, not unto themselves, 'but unto him which died for them, and rose again' (2 Corinthians 5:15). There was a day when they sought to live for themselves and for the world, but now they seek to live unto the Lord. And therefore we read that they have a work of faith and a labour of love, and patience of hope. Their work of faith *is* a labour of love, for 'faith without works is dead', and they are constrained by love to seek to work for the Lord. They need to be patient in connection with the work that they have, for we read, 'Let us not be weary in well doing: for in due season we shall reap, if we faint not' (Galatians 6:9). 'Therefore, my beloved brethren, be ye stedfast, unmoveable, always abounding in the work of the Lord, forasmuch as ye know that your labour is not in vain in the Lord' (1 Corinthians 15:58).

Those who have this lively hope seek to purify themselves as he is pure. They seek to be cleansed and sanctified. Their hope lays hold on Christ as the forerunner who has entered within the veil, 'even Jesus, made an high priest for ever after the order of Melchisedec' (Hebrews 6:20). They look to him as a Saviour. He is an advocate within the veil. 'And if any man sin, we have an advocate with the Father, Jesus Christ the righteous: and he is the propitiation for our sins: and not for ours only, but also for the sins of the whole world' (1 John 2:1–2).

3. The blessings bound up with the lively hope

Then we have the blessings which are bound up with this hope. Those who have this lively hope are found waiting with expectation upon the Lord. They seek to live, not for themselves, but for the Lord. They are 'begotten again'—born again. Their hope is the fruit of the new birth. It is the exercise of the new nature. 'They that wait upon the LORD shall renew their strength; they shall mount up with wings as eagles; they shall run, and not be weary; and they shall walk, and not faint' (Isaiah 40:31). This people seek the blessings that are in Christ Jesus.

That is a fruit of their being born again and sanctified, sprinkled with the blood of Christ and washed with the washing of regeneration. They have the obedience of faith, and that shows that they have Christ in them as the hope of glory. Those who have this hope are persons who have been justified, and they are being sanctified, and they shall yet be glorified. At death they shall enter into this inheritance 'incorruptible, and undefiled, and that fadeth not away'.

This inheritance is 'reserved in heaven' for them. It is secured for them in the purpose of God—prepared for them before the foundation of the world, secured by Christ's blood and Christ's intercession. He is interceding on their behalf, that they might be sanctified through the Truth, and kept from the evil that is in the world, and at last glorified. It is only through his intercession that they are kept.

The proof that this inheritance has been reserved for them is the living desire that they have in their souls. It is as sure an evidence as a copy of the title deeds to a property. As we read, 'If they had been mindful of that country from whence they came out, they might have had opportunity to have returned. But now they desire a better country, that is, an heavenly: wherefore God is not ashamed to be called their God: for he hath prepared for them a city' (Hebrews 11:15–16).

They prove they are his people by not returning to the country from which they came. If their hearts were in that country, they would return. That was true of Orpah. Although outwardly she appeared as promising as Ruth, she showed clearly that she was mindful of her native country. Her heart was still in Moab, and when the opportunity presented itself she went back—back to the country from whence she came, back to her gods and to idolatry.

That was true of Lot's wife too. Although she appeared promising, she was mindful of the country out of which she came. She looked back, and to all appearances began to go back. Her heart was in Sodom.

But although those who have this lively hope have opportunities presented to them of going back, it is when they are tried that they show that they have a desire after 'a better country, that is, an heavenly'. They know there is nothing for them in going back to the country out of which they came, to the light that they had in the days of their ignorance. They cannot go back, although they will be tempted to do so. In these circumstances they show that they have a living desire, that their hope is toward something better.

The Lord's people feel ashamed of themselves, and their confession is, 'To us belongeth confusion of face' (Daniel 9:8). But the Lord declares that he is not ashamed to be called their God; he has prepared a city for them, 'a city which hath foundations, whose builder and maker is God' (Hebrews 11:10). He makes known that he has reserved this for them. And the confession of those who have the living desire is, 'The LORD is my portion, saith my soul; therefore will I hope in him' (Lamentations 3:24).

This people are conscious of their need of being kept: they cannot keep themselves. They are 'kept by the power of God through faith unto salvation' (1 Peter 1:5). They exercise faith upon him as the keeper of Israel who 'slumbers not, nor sleeps', as the one who is able to keep them from falling.

It is at death that they shall receive the fulness of God's salvation, when their souls shall be made perfect in holiness. Meantime their prayer is: 'Hold up my goings, Lord, me guide / in those thy paths divine, / so that my footsteps may not slide / out of those ways of thine' (Psalm 17:5).

On their wilderness journey, they came to entertain a good hope through grace, and they came to follow the Saviour and to realise their need of being kept by him. Between that time and the time of entering upon their inheritance we read that on their wilderness journey they are oftentimes 'in heaviness through manifold temptations' (verse 6). There is a need for the trials through which they pass, 'that the trial of your faith, being much more precious than of gold that perisheth, though it be tried with fire, might be found unto praise and honour and glory at the appearing of Jesus Christ' (verse 7).

It is when their faith is tried that Christ becomes precious to them. They show that they have love to him by looking to him: it is to him they cleave when they are tried. But although they are tried by manifold temptations, they are kept by the power of God. He will not suffer them to be tried above that which they are able to bear, and they shall go from strength to strength until at length they appear before the Lord in Zion.

I have recounted before now the parable used by a godly minister of the past, the Rev. John Macrae, in a sermon that he preached on Solomon's chariot.[10] Solomon's char-

---

[10] John Macrae (1794–1876), known popularly as 'Big Macrae' (Gaelic: *Mac-Rath Mòr*), was successively minister in the Black Isle, Greenock, Lochs, and Carloway. The sermon was first published in a Gaelic biography in 1894, issued the following year in English translation: Nicol Nicolson, *The Reverend John MacRae of Knockbain, Greenock, and Lewis: A short account of his life and fragments of his preaching* (Inverness: Young, 1895).

iot, he said, is the chariot of the everlasting gospel. Christ, the New Testament Solomon, is in the chariot and the Holy Spirit is the driver. In going through the wilderness of this world, they found one by the roadside bemoaning the hardness of his heart. How hard his heart was! Because of this he was in heaviness and cast down, and Christ said to the Holy Spirit, 'Stop, blessed driver, and bring him into the chariot.'

And in this way Macrae went on to enumerate the different trials which those who have this good hope suffer, for these are the complaints of the living in Jerusalem. The Lord will meet their needs and uphold them. 'They go from strength to strength, every one of them in Zion appeareth before God' (Psalm 84:7). They are kept by his power and they look to him alone. 'Thou, with thy counsel, while I live, / wilt me conduct and guide; / and to thy glory afterward / receive me to abide' (Psalm 73:24).

They are a blessed people who have this hope. 'Happy art thou, O Israel: who is like unto thee, a people saved by the LORD!' (Deuteronomy 33:29).

Christ is set before us as the only hope—as a door of hope—in the everlasting gospel, and we are invited to him. He himself invites us: 'Come unto me, all ye that labour and are heavy laden, and I will give you rest. Take my yoke upon you, and learn of me; for I am meek and lowly in heart: and ye shall find rest unto your souls. For my yoke is easy, and my burden is light' (Matthew 11:28–30).

May he bless his Truth.

The more sure word of prophecy

We have also a more sure word of prophecy;
whereunto ye do well that ye take heed, as unto
a light that shineth in a dark place, until the day
dawn, and the day star arise in your hearts.

2 PETER 1:19

IN the first place we may make a few remarks about what we are to understand by 'the sure word of prophecy'. In the second place we shall consider the people who make this profession, the 'we' of our text. In the third place we may notice the exhortation given them: 'Whereunto ye do well that ye take heed, as unto a light that shineth in a dark place.' And in the last place, we shall notice the day that is to dawn for this people: 'Until the day dawn, and the day star arise in your hearts.' That is the dawn of an eternal day, the dawn of eternal bliss in Immanuel's land.

1. The sure word of prophecy

By the 'sure word of prophecy' we are to understand the Word of God—the scriptures of the Old and New Testaments. 'The prophecy came not in old time by the will of man, but holy men of God spake as they were moved by the Holy Ghost' (2 Peter 1:21). It is to the sure word of prophecy—to God's revealed will, as we have that in the scriptures of the Old and New Testaments—that the apostle Peter is here directing the attention of his hearers. He is calling upon them to give heed to this Word as a 'light that shineth in a dark place', for all spiritual light can be obtained only from the Scriptures, this 'sure word of prophecy'.

It is in connection with confirming and establishing the doctrine of the second coming of Christ that the apostle is here directing their attention to the sure word of prophecy. And he is directing the attention of the Church of God to the end of time to what the sure word of prophecy has to say about this doctrine. There were those who regarded the doctrine of the second coming as a cunningly devised fable. 'Scoffers, walking after their own lusts, and saying, Where is the promise of his coming? for since the fathers fell asleep, all things continue as they were from the beginning of the creation' (2 Peter 3:3–4). It is to refute the false ideas of these scoffers that the apostle confirms the doctrine of the second coming of the Lord Jesus Christ, and he directs the attention of his hearers (and of the church of God to the end of time) to what the sure word of prophecy says regarding this doctrine.

Peter says that although his hearers were already 'established in the present truth', yet he would 'not be negligent to put you always in remembrance of these things' (verse 12). We are to hear these truths again and again, even if we are already established in them. The apostle Peter thought it meet to put them always in remembrance of these things. He was not questioning their sincerity or their knowledge, but he thought meet, 'as long as I am in this tabernacle, to stir you up by putting you in remembrance' (verse 13). We are so prone to let slip what we hear. We need to be reminded again and again of the great truths of the everlasting gospel.

At this time, although Peter believed that those to whom he was writing knew this doctrine and were established in the truth of it, he sees it proper and fitting that he should bring it again to their remembrance because of the denials that were abroad concerning this holy doctrine, and because of scoffers who were looking upon it as a cunningly devised fable.

The proof he brings forward of the second coming of Christ at the great day of judgment is the transfiguration. Peter, along with James and John, his fellow apostles, were eyewitnesses of the transfiguration. 'We made known unto you the power and coming of our Lord Jesus Christ ... for he received from God the Father honour and glory, when there came such a voice to him from the excellent glory, This is my beloved Son, in whom I am well pleased. And this voice which came from heaven we heard, when we were with him in the holy mount.' On the Mount of Transfiguration, in the days of his humiliation, Jesus was transfigured before them. His face shone as the sun and his raiment became white as the light, he received honour and glory from God the Father.

Peter here says that he and his fellow apostles James and John were eyewitnesses of this. They beheld his glory, 'the glory as of the only begotten of the Father, full of grace and truth' (John 1:14). They heard the voice of God the Father testifying, 'This is my beloved Son, in whom I am well pleased.' Peter describes Christ's majesty, when the glory of his eternal deity shone through his manhood. The transfiguration confirms not only his eternal deity and many other doctrines, it is also proof that he will come again the second time in power and glory. He received honour and glory from the Father on the Mount of Transfiguration, and Peter and James and John were eye-witnesses of his majesty on the holy mount. However, at his second coming—at the great day of judgment—he shall come in the glory of his Father. He will be glorified in his human nature with the glory which he had with the Father before the world was, and every eye shall see him.

Under divine inspiration, this is one of the proofs with which the apostle Peter confirms the doctrine of the second coming of Christ, and refutes the arguments of scoffers who regarded it as a cunningly devised fable.

Those to whom he writes were not eyewitnesses of the transfiguration, but they had the Scriptures. And in case they might question what he says, he refers them to the Scriptures, especially to the Scriptures of the Old Testament, for the canon of the New was not complete at this time. He refers to these Scriptures as 'a more sure word of prophecy'. If they would give good heed to these Scriptures, they would see how the prophecies regarding Christ's first coming were fulfilled: the place of his birth, the tribe he was to spring from, the place of his birth, the manner of his birth, the time of his birth, the miracles he was to perform in the days of his flesh, and his sufferings and his death and his resurrection. All these were in the Old Testament Scriptures. And because they were the very Word of God, they were therefore sure.

In Old Testament times, people might have regarded the first coming of Christ in the flesh—the great mystery of godliness, God manifest in the flesh—as being a cunningly devised fable. But when all these prophecies were fulfilled to the letter in connection with the first coming of Christ, that made the prophecy more sure, as it were. It put these prophecies beyond any doubt. Their fulfilment confirmed the prophecies as true.

The prophecies regarding Christ's second coming at the great day of judgment are also in the Bible, which is as a light shining in a dark place. It is the Word of God that gives light on Christ's second coming. Those to whom Peter writes were not eyewitnesses of the Saviour's glory. But if they took good heed to the Scriptures they could be convinced that, as surely as the prophecies concerning Christ's first coming in the flesh were fulfilled, so surely would the prophecies concerning his second advent be fulfilled. His transfiguration was a prophecy of his second coming, when he shall appear in the glory of his Father, just as his resurrection from the dead is a prophecy and a proof of the final resurrection—the resurrection of the just and the unjust.

Peter says that they had need to take heed to this sure word of prophecy 'as unto a light that shineth in a dark place' in connection with this as well as other doctrines. He thinks it meet 'to stir you up by putting you in re-membrance' although they were already established in these truths. And if it was necessary for the saints to whom he was writing, how much more is it necessary in our day! This doctrine of the second coming of Christ is denied in our day as surely as it was denied in the day of the apostle. There are scoffers in our day, who deny not only this doctrine but every doctrine of the Truth.

Yet it is not so much the open denial of this doctrine which has appeared in our day, but a perversion of it. False interpretations have been put upon this doctrine of Christ's second coming: views that have sprung up in the last hundred years or so, and that have spread through the world like a flood, so that you can hardly read any so-called evangelical magazine or literature nowadays without coming across these teachings. Great emphasis is laid upon the second coming of the Lord, how he is to come and to reign in this world, and so on. The so-called evangelical literature of our day is saturated with an interpretation of this doctrine which is not in accordance with God's Word. The doctrine is believed, but wrongly interpreted, and there is therefore a need that we be established in this truth.

Although the apostle knew that those to whom he wrote were established in this truth, he saw fit to put them in remembrance. What is the point of harping on these matters? Because this doctrine of the second coming is greatly perverted, wrongly interpreted, in our day.

The Seventh Day Adventists, for example, are a powerful sect numerically and financially. One of their founders, William Miller, wrote about the second coming, and from his calculations Christ was to come in 1844. Well, 1844 came and passed, and Christ did not come. But Mrs Ellen White stepped into the breach and said William Miller was quite correct, but he had been mistaken in believing Christ was to come back to earth in 1844. She said what happened was that in 1844 Christ entered into the heavenly sanctuary to complete the atonement and to cleanse the upper sanctuary. When he had completed the atonement and cleansed the upper sanctuary, then he would come back to earth. That is the heretical, blasphemous teaching of Mrs Ellen White on Christ's second coming. There are thousands upon thousands who believe that.

Then we come to the Jehovah's Witnesses. What a powerful sect they are! Thousands and millions have been deluded by that sect. Their Pastor Russell also gave a prominent place to the second coming. He said that Christ came to the earth in 1874, and that through this he himself was enlightened to propound certain doctrines. His successor, Judge Rutherford, gave as truth that Christ came in 1874 to America. His proofs of this were these inventions: bicycles, cream separators, vacuum cleaners, submarines. skyscrapers, telephones, railway signals, typewriters, cash registers, celluloid, match machines, barbed wire, aeroplanes, artificial dyes, and so on.

These are the proofs, the so-called spiritual proofs, that Judge Rutherford offered of Christ coming back to America in 1874. He also prophesied that there would be a resurrection in 1925. He built a mansion in San Diego in California for Abraham, Isaac and Jacob, and put an expensive car in the garage, so that Abraham, Isaac and Jacob could stay in the mansion and tour the States. Well, Rutherford died in 1942, the mansion was sold, and thus ended another false prophecy.

But more subtle and dangerous are the interpretations given in the Scofield Bible by the dispensationalists. Persons professing to be evangelical, and often Calvinistic in their views, are taken in by these. There are many premillenarians who will have nothing to do with dispensationalism. There are thousands of Arminians who will have nothing to do with it. At the same time it is a plausible interpretation and thousands are deceived by dispensationalism.

Their views on the second coming get a prominent place in their literature. They believe, of course, that Christ is coming back at what they call the 'rapture' to carry away his people from this world, not only those of his people alive in this world, but the dead. 'Rapture' means to carry away. The saints who are dead are to be resurrected, and the living and the dead are to be suddenly and silently raptured caught up to meet the Lord in the air. They maintain this will take place at least a thousand years before the last day. It will take place at any moment, and they are waiting, expecting that at any moment—perhaps when they are taking breakfast in the morning or before they go to bed at night—they may find themselves with the Lord in the sky.

They hold that the Lord's people are to be in the sky for seven years with Christ. During these seven years the 'tribulation' begins in this world, and it is during the 'tribulation' that the Antichrist is to appear. According to them, the Antichrist is not yet come. He is some future monster who is to appear during the 'tribulation'.

Scofield adapted and popularised this view about the Antichrist, but the person who first propounded it was a Jesuit priest called Luis del Alcázar,[11] to divert the attention of people from what the Reformers were saying, that the papacy was the Antichrist and the man of sin the son

---

[11] A Spanish Jesuit theologian, also known as Ludovicus ab Alcasar or Louis of Alcazar (1554–1613).

of perdition. This Jesuit invented the theory—and tried to confirm it from the book of Revelation—that the Anti-christ was to appear in the distant future at the time of the tribulation. And Darby, one of the founders of the Breth-ren, adapted that view concerning the Antichrist and popularised it, as did Scofield and also the High Church party in the Church of England, whose policy of course is union with Rome. This view suits their policy very well.

Dispensationalists following the Scofield Bible do not be-lieve what we have in the Reformed confessions, that the pope is the Antichrist. They believe the Antichrist is to appear during the tribulation. They also believe that dur-ing the tribulation the Jews are to be converted. And the remarkable thing is that they are not to be converted through the outpouring of the Holy Spirit as the Word of God declares, because dispensationalists teach that the Ho-ly Spirit is taken from the earth when the rapture takes place. Along with the saints, the Holy Spirit is taken away, and he is no longer in the world. But the Jews are to be converted, they say, through seeing Christ standing on the Mount of Olives, and that will be the means of their con-version.

The Jews, so this theory holds, are to be converted at the mere sight of Christ, their Messiah, on the Mount of Ol-ives—that is, when he shall come back to stand on the earth—and through their testimony whole nations are to be converted. We must point out, however, that people were not converted at the mere sight of Jesus at the time of his first advent, and that it is the particular work of the Holy Spirit to regenerate the soul and give it new vision, and so enable it to turn to Christ. The mere presence of Christ often had the effect of hardening his enemies rather than converting them. But, according to the dispensation-alists, at this time the Jews will be converted, and they will be the means of converting millions of the Gentiles, and that will be without the Holy Spirit. How could they be regenerated if there were no Holy Spirit present to give them the new birth? The whole theory is thoroughly un-scriptural throughout, since it would by inference deny that man is dead in sins, and thus contradict Ephesians 2:1. And then, at the end of the seventy years, after Christ and his people and the saints that were resurrected have been in the sky, they are to come back to this world. Christ is to reign in Jerusalem and mingle with all the converted Jews and with the converted Gentiles, and then the king-dom is to be set up. They do not believe that Christ's kingdom is yet set up: it will not be set up till then.

These are some of the different views held in connection with the second coming of Christ. According to the Truth, however, Christ will come again 'at the last day'. 'This is the Father's will which hath sent me, that of all which he hath given me I should lose nothing, but should raise it up again at the last day. And this is the will of him that sent me, that every one which seeth the Son, and believeth on him, may have everlasting life: and I will raise him up at the last day' (John 6:39–40). 'No man can come to me except the Father which hath sent me draw him: and I will raise him up at the last day' (John 6:44). 'Whoso eateth my flesh, and drinketh my blood, hath eternal life; and I will raise him up at the last day' (John 6:54). Martha said to the Saviour about Lazarus that she knew he would rise again at the resurrection on the last day.

The resurrection, when Christ will come in the glory of his Father, is at the last day. The Truth speaks of the judgment at the last day, when the devils shall be judged. They are at present reserved in chains of darkness against the judgment of the last day. It is at the last day that Christ will raise his people and all who believe in him, as he emphatically declares in the sixth chapter of John.

Teachings about the rapture and so on are just fanciful interpretations of the Scriptures. For many, this view of the second coming is the main feature of their religion. But the second coming is when Christ will come in the glory of his Father with the holy angels at the last day 'to judge the world in righteousness, / justice to give each one'.

Before that time there will be a worldwide spiritual resurrection, comparable to the literal resurrection at the day of judgment, when the Holy Spirit shall be poured forth and when multitudes shall be turned to the Saviour. The fulness of the Gentiles shall be brought in and the ingathering of the Jews shall take place, as life from the dead.

The apostle Peter commends those to whom he writes for taking heed to this doctrine.

2. The people who have the sure word of prophecy

In the second place we shall consider the 'we' of our text. The apostle includes himself among these people, for whom a day is to dawn. They are to give good heed to the word of prophecy, as to a light that shines in a dark place 'until the day dawn, and the day star arise in your hearts'.

They are to hold fast, however dark the present day may be, and however much apostasy there may be from the Truth, through fanciful interpretations of the Truth and persons taken aside from their stedfastness. He bids them beware: 'Ye therefore, brethren beloved, seeing ye know these things before, beware lest ye also, being led away with the error of the wicked, fall from your own stedfastness. But grow in grace, and in the knowledge of our Lord and Saviour Jesus Christ. To him be glory both now and for ever. Amen.' (2 Peter 5:17–18).

These people are duty bound to search the Scriptures, to read the Scriptures in private as well as at family worship. I have mentioned before what a godly minister in Scotland said, that in the dust on some people's Bibles you could write the words 'eternal damnation'. They never search their Bibles. Yet this is the sure word of prophecy that can make us wise unto salvation. 'By what means shall a young man learn / his way to purify? / If he according to thy word / thereto attentive be' (Psalm 119:9).

We read that 'the righteous hath a hope in his death' (Proverbs 14:52) and 'the path of the just is as the shining light, that shineth more and more unto the perfect day' (Proverbs 4:18). Those for whom this day will dawn have a hope in their death. The apostle writes to them as those 'that have obtained like precious faith with us through the righteousness of God and our Saviour Jesus Christ'. It is those who have this saving faith that will have this fulfilled in their soul's experience. In the dark valley of the shadow of death, the day star shall arise in their hearts, and that shall be the beginning of an eternal day for them. Then the promise shall be fulfilled in its fulness: 'Thy sun shall no more go down; neither shall thy moon withdraw itself:

for the LORD shall be thine everlasting light, and the days of thy mourning shall be ended' (Isaiah 60:20).

We may make a few remarks on the persons who have this faith—the 'like precious faith with us'. Peter does not say that they were eyewitnesses of Christ's majesty, as he and James and John were on the Mount of Transfiguration. That was a special revelation given to only these three of the disciples. Peter does not make that special revelation a standard, as it were, for other people. The Lord gives a greater revelation of himself to some of his people than he gives to others. But what the Lord in his sovereignty may give to the one and withhold from the other is not the standard. And for a person to make a standard for his own conversion and the manner of it, is contrary to the Scriptures. Regarding the new birth the Lord says, 'The wind bloweth where it listeth, and thou hearest the sound thereof, but canst not tell whence it cometh, and whither it goeth: so is every one that is born of the Spirit' (John 5:8). There is a mystery in connection with it. And where faith is implanted and new life given to the soul, that soul makes its faith known in the life and conversation. 'By their fruits ye shall know them.'

It is not of special revelations that the apostle makes a standard in this epistle. He says that they have one thing in common, and that is 'like precious faith'. They may not have it in the same measure or the same degree, for there is weak faith and there is strong faith. But whoever has faith will be saved, for faith, however weak it may be in its motions, unites the sinner to the Lord Jesus Christ. Where there is faith, he is the object of faith, and by faith a sinner rests upon Christ alone for salvation. What is faith? As the Shorter Catechism puts it, 'Faith in Jesus

231

Christ is a saving grace, whereby we receive and rest upon him alone for salvation, as he is offered to us in the gospel.'

Those who have it receive the righteousness of God in our Saviour Jesus Christ. This is the channel through which they receive the gift of faith. There could be no faith bestowed upon the race of sinners to which we belong apart from the righteousness of our God and Saviour Jesus Christ. It is in virtue of that eternal righteousness—the work which he finished in his obedience unto death—that the gift of faith is bestowed upon any sinner. Those who have this faith are brought to see that their faith is not on the grounds of their own righteousness. Their confession is, 'Not by works of righteousness which we have done, but according to his mercy he saved us, by the washing of regeneration, and renewing of the Holy Ghost; which he shed on us abundantly through Jesus Christ our Saviour' (Titus 3:5–6).

Those who have this saving faith are brought to see themselves lost and condemned, and to know that they could not save themselves, and that they have nothing with which to pay their debt. It is when Christ is revealed to the soul that the soul is made able and willing to close in with Christ as he is freely offered in the everlasting gospel. And what is it to receive a faith's view of Christ? What is it to see Christ by faith? I will offer you Jonathan Edwards' scriptural definition. 'It is not to get a vision of Christ with the bodily eye, or to see some bodily shape. That is not a faith's view of Christ. It is to see the excellency of Christ, the suitability of Christ, and the all-sufficiency of Christ, and to see the way of salvation through him in one's heart, for with the heart man believeth unto righteousness and with the mouth confession is made unto salvation' (Romans 10:10). The soul is enabled to go forth out of itself, as it were, unto Christ, and to rest in Christ and to trust in him.

Can you trace that in your spiritual experience? A time or a moment, however brief, when your lost and hell-deserving soul went forth and rested in Christ? When Christ and your soul met? For saving faith, which is of the Holy Spirit's operation, brings Christ and the soul near. The soul comes to rest in Christ. Whoever has not this saving faith—whatever else he may have—is still in the gall of bitterness and in the bond of iniquity.

This faith is precious because God is the author of it. It is precious because Christ is its object. 'Unto you therefore which believe he is precious.' He is precious in his person and in his offices as prophet, priest and king.

This faith needs Christ in all his offices. However weak the faith may be, and however much the person may be in doubt as to whether he has truly and sincerely closed in with Christ, Christ is precious to that person as prophet, priest, and king. It is as a prophet, priest and king that Christ saves the soul, that he has power on earth to forgive sin. Faith goes forth to Christ as the one who can cleanse the soul from sin. Those who have this faith say with the Psalmist, 'Do thou with hyssop sprinkle me, / I shall be cleansed so; / yea, wash thou me, and then I shall / be whiter than the snow' (Psalm 51:7).

This faith is precious in its exercise and in its fruits. It is not a dead faith. All that pertains to Christ becomes precious to that person. He seeks to uphold the cause of Christ. He has a heart attachment to the cause of Christ, however poor he may be. His desire is that the cause of Christ would flourish, that his kingdom would come—in his own soul, and in his family, and to the ends of the earth. He has a heart to support the cause of Christ. The noted Archibald Cook said that the person who would go to hell never got a mind to support the cause of Christ. But those who have this faith have a heart to support his cause. They also have a love to his day. They have a love to his people. 'We show that we have passed from death unto life, because we love the brethren' (1 John 3:14). They have taken the Word of God as a lamp to their feet, and they take good heed to this 'more sure word of prophecy' as to 'a light that shineth in a dark place'. It is the Word of God that can give them light on their duty, and on the way that they should take. This world is in darkness, and all the light of this world's science and philosophy cannot give spiritual light or spiritual life to your soul. You can only obtain this spiritual light from the 'sure word of prophecy'.

3. The exhortation to take good heed

God's people are here called on to take good heed to the Scriptures, so that they might be well established in the Truth, so that they will be able to give a reason for the hope that is in them, so that they might know how to gainsay the adversary and so that they might know the doctrines of the Word of God and how people might pervert the doctrines, so that they might defend them.

Many a person knew these doctrines and even preached them, and yet they were bewitched and taken aside from their stedfastness. So the apostle cautions, 'Ye, therefore, beloved, seeing ye know these things before, beware lest

234

ye also, being led away with the error of the wicked, fall from your own stedfastness. But grow in grace, and in the knowledge of our Lord and Saviour Jesus Christ' (2 Peter 3:17–18). The Lord's people are to be going forth in the footsteps of the flock, however spectacular other ways may be. Far from being bewitched by fanciful interpretations and taken up with them as many people are, they are to give good heed to the sure word of prophecy and to seek to give the obedience of faith. It is in following the footsteps of the flock that we shall find food for our souls and light for our souls.

Hear the plaint of the true church of God. 'Tell me, O thou whom my soul loveth, where thou feedest, where thou makest thy flock to rest at noon: for why should I be as one that turneth aside by the flocks of thy companions?' (Song of Solomon 1:7). She is not getting the food and rest for her soul that she desires. The Lord answers her: 'If thou know not, O thou fairest among women, go thy way forth by the footsteps of the flock.' She is to be a follower of them who through faith and patience are now inheriting the promises, of those who in their day and generation were faithful unto death in following the Good Shepherd.

We are to walk in obedience to the doctrines of the Westminster Confession of Faith and the Canons of Dort. There we have set before us doctrinally the footsteps of the flock.

4. The dawn of the eternal day

In the last place, consider the day that is to dawn for them: 'Until the day dawn, and the day star arise in your hearts.' The Lord's people are at times in darkness, and especially in a dark day. A godly minister of the past said that in a dark day the Lord's true people could hardly get beyond 'I hope' and 'I trust.' Not that he was saying that there were no persons who received a full assurance of their interest in Christ, but for the most part, when the Spirit is withheld, the Lord's people are weak. They are weak in the faith. They do not attain that stature and stability and eminence to which the godly of the past attained.

But in the darkness, they are to give heed to this 'sure word of prophecy' and to seek to conform to his Word. Whatever darkness they may be in, and whatever assaults the prince of darkness may make on their souls as they enter the valley of the shadow of death, the day is to dawn. They may be in darkness and may be tempest-tossed with fears that perhaps, after all, they will come short. That is a concern of those who have this faith: they are concerned about their state. The matter is too momentous to take things for granted, but this is the promise: the day *will* dawn, and the day star *will* arise in their hearts. Christ speaks of himself as 'the root and the offspring of David, and the bright and morning star' (Revelation 22:16). He is the root of David as to his deity; he is the offspring of David as to his humanity. He has the two natures in the one person, and that for ever. The morning star is the harbinger of day, and no matter what darkness Christ's people may have, at death Christ will arise in their hearts as the morning star.

That shall be the dawn of an endless day for them. Sorrow and sighing shall flee away. That promise shall be fulfilled: 'Thy sun shall no more go down; neither shall thy moon withdraw itself; for the LORD shall be thine everlasting light, and the days of thy mourning shall be ended.'

They are travelling towards this place. And as Moses said to Hobab, when the children of Israel were journeying toward the land of Canaan, 'We are journeying unto the place of which the LORD said, I will give it you: come thou with us, and we will do thee good: for the LORD hath spoken good concerning Israel' (Numbers 10:29).

May he bless his Truth.